revise

GCSE
German

Sarah Boote and Sheila Hunt

with Tony Buzan

HIGHCLIFFE SCHOOL
Parkside, Highcliffe
Christchurch
Dorset BH23 4QD

Hodder & Stoughton

A MEMBER OF THE HODDER HEADLINE GROUP

Every picture tells a story

 Just as a 'hole in the wall' keeps your money safe and ready to hand when you need it, we hope that you will look on our 'Wortautomat' as your 'hole in the wall' vocabulary bank account. There is of course one very important difference: the 'Wortautomat' never runs out, and the more you use it, the bigger your balance becomes! Feel free, therefore, to dip into it whenever you like, and watch your vocabulary increase.

 Frau Grün keeps everyone in order with the help of a smart tap with her rolling pin, and you are no exception! Frau Grün has learnt from bitter experience the mistakes and difficulties which the learner can encounter, so her rolling pin is there to warn you of the unexpected, and to help you avoid trouble.

 For Martin Müller no meal is complete unless smothered in lashings of tomato ketchup. His icon shows you how to add just that little something which will lift your answer out of the ordinary and give the examiner a nice surprise, and you a few more marks. **Enjoy your meal**!

Acknowledgments The authors and publishers would like to thank Gudrun and Werner Knoblauch for reading final proofs, and Caroline Woods for the Essential Starting Points material.

ISBN 0 340 71145 0

First published 1998
Impression number   10 9 8 7 6 5 4 3 2 1
Year   2002 2001 2000 1999 1998

The 'Teach Yourself' name and logo are registered trade marks of Hodder & Stoughton Ltd.

Copyright © 1998 Sarah Boote and Sheila Hunt
Introduction ('Revision made easy') © 1998 Tony Buzan

All rights reserved. No part of this publication may be reproduced or transmitted in any form or by any means, electronic or mechanical, including photocopy, recording, or any information storage and retrieval system, without permission in writing from the publisher or under licence from the Copyright Licensing Agency Limited. Further details of such licences (for reprographic reproduction) may be obtained from the Copyright Licensing Agency Limited, of 90 Tottenham Court Road, London W1P 9HE.

Designed and produced by Gecko Ltd, Bicester, Oxon
Printed in Great Britain for Hodder & Stoughton Educational, a division of Hodder Headline Plc, 338 Euston Road, London NW1 3BH by Scotprint Ltd, Musselburgh, Scotland.

Mind Maps: Peter Bull
Illustrations: Richard Duszczak

Cover design: Amanda Hawkes
Cover illustration: Paul Bateman

Contents

Revision made easy	5
Essential starting points	9

1 He Leute! 15
Self, family, friends, pets, hobbies and interests.
All about Marlene	15
Neighbours from hell	20
Creature comforts	22
Martin's magnetic charm	23
Test yourself tasks:	
1 Listening	23
2 Listening	24
3 Speaking	24
4 Speaking	24

2 Bei uns 25
House and home, jobs round the house and pocket money.
Greenhouse gas	25
Slave labour	29
Test yourself tasks:	
1 Speaking	32
2 Reading	32

3 Zu Besuch 33
On a visit, eating habits and entertainment at home.
Gabi checks in	33
Couch potatoes	35
Test yourself tasks:	
1 Listening	38
2 Speaking	39
3 Speaking	39
4 Speaking	39
5 Reading	39
6 Reading	39
7 Writing	40
8 Writing	40

4 Schule stinkt! 41
School routine, subjects, facilities, activities, rules and uniform.
Day in the life …	41
English spoken here	43
School rules!	44

Test yourself tasks:	
1 Speaking	48
2 Reading	48
3 Reading	48

5 An die Arbeit 49
Jobs, work experience, further education and training, and phone calls.
Just the job	49
Experience needed	51
Test yourself tasks:	
1 Listening	55
2 Speaking	55
3 Speaking	56
4 Writing	56
5 Writing	56

6 Die Stadt ruft 57
Home town, directions, shopping and illness.
Market forces	57
Now swallow that!	61
High Street Blues	63
Test yourself tasks:	
1 Speaking	66
2 Speaking	66
3 Speaking	67
4 Writing	67

7 Freizeit macht Spaß! 68
Going out, restaurants, cinema, theatre, sport and lost property.
Persuasion	68
Men in tights	70
Brief encounter	71
Dating the enemy	74
Test yourself tasks:	
1 Listening	76
2 Listening	77
3 Speaking	77
4 Speaking	77

8 Los geht's! 78
Holidays, booking accommodation, weather, accidents, transport, buying petrol and car breakdowns.
Different strokes	78

Base instinct	83
Heavy weather	84
At your service	86
Hit and miss	87
Ticket to ride	89
Home alone	90
Test yourself tasks:	
1 Speaking	91
2 Speaking	92
3 Reading	92

9 Putting it all together   93
List of frequent exam question instructions, exam hints and Mind Map check lists of syllabus requirements.

Making sense of the instructions and rubrics	93
Areas of Experience	93
A Everyday activities	94
B Personal and social	95
C The world around us	96
D The world of work	97
E The international world	98

10 Meet the Memory Joggers   99
Your personal fitness programme in Mind Maps and other pictures.
Everything you need to peak for the examination day.

What time is it?	100
What time of year is it?	101
How many?	102
Where did you come?	102
What is the weather like?	103
Where do you live?	104
What is it like?	105
What colour is it?	106
Who's in your family?	107
How do you help at home?	108
What do you do in your spare time?	109
What would you like?	110
What fruit and vegetables are there?	111
What are you buying?	112
What are you wearing?	113
What's wrong?	114
Where does it hurt?	115
Which way?	116
Where is…?	116
Where are you from?	117
What do you speak?	118
What do you learn?	119
What is your school like?	120
What do you do on holiday?	121
What question words?	122
How does the alphabet sound?	122
'Do it yourself'	123

11 Grammar   125
Just a few ideas cooked up by Frau Grün to make German grammar easier to swallow.

Frau Grün gets to grips with grammar	125
1 Nouns	126
2 Cases	129
3 Adjectives	130
4 Adverbs	131
5 Adjectives: comparative / superlative	132
6 Adverbs: comparative / superlative	132
7 Prepositions	133
8 Verbs	135
9 Tenses	139
10 Word order	143
11 Conjunctions	145

12 Mock Exam   146
Further hints in exam preparation and practice exam questions along with answers and marking schemes.

Exam hints	146
Speaking	148
Listening	148
Reading	150
Writing	154

13 Effective revision or too much television?   156
Tante Inge's problem page
Ten fun ways to revise

Index   159

Revision made easy

The four pages that follow contain a gold mine of information on how you can achieve success both at school and in your exams. Read them and apply the information, and you will be able to spend less, but more efficient, time studying, with better results. If you already have another *Hodder & Stoughton Revision Guide*, skim-read these pages to remind yourself about the exciting new techniques the books use, then move ahead to page 9.

This section gives you vital information on how to remember more *while* you are learning and how to remember more *after* you have finished studying. It explains

- how to use special techniques to improve your memory
- how to use a revolutionary note-taking technique called Mind Maps that will double your memory and help you to write essays, use the language and answer exam questions
- how to read everything faster while at the same time improving your comprehension and concentration

All this information is packed into the next four pages, so make sure you read them!

Your *amazing* memory

There are five important things you must know about your brain and memory to revolutionise your school life.

1. how your memory ('recall') works *while* you are learning
2. how your memory works *after* you have finished learning
3. how to use Mind Maps – a special technique for helping you with all aspects of your studies
4. how to increase your reading speed
5. how to zap your revision

1 Recall *during* learning – the need for breaks

When you are studying, your memory can concentrate, understand and remember well for between 20 and 45 minutes at a time. Then it *needs* a break. If you carry on for longer than this without one, your memory starts to break down! If you study for hours non-stop, you will remember only a fraction of what you have been trying to learn, and you will have wasted valuable revision time.

So, ideally, *study for less than an hour*, then take a five- to ten-minute break. During the break listen to music, go for a walk, do some exercise, or just daydream. (Daydreaming is a necessary brain-power booster – geniuses do it regularly.) During the break your brain will be sorting out what it has been learning, and you will go back to your books with the new information safely stored and organised in your memory banks. We recommend breaks at regular intervals as you work through the *Revision Guides*. Make sure you take them!

2 Recall *after* learning – the waves of your memory

What do you think begins to happen to your memory straight *after* you have finished learning something? Does it immediately start forgetting? No! Your brain actually *increases* its power and carries on remembering. For a short time after your study session, your brain integrates the information, making a more complete picture of everything it has just learnt. Only then does the rapid decline in memory begin, and as much as 80 per cent of what you have learnt can be forgotten in a day.

However, if you catch the top of the wave of your memory, and briefly review (look back over) what you have been revising at the correct time, the memory is stamped in far more strongly, and stays at the crest of the wave for a much longer time. To maximise your brain's power to remember, take a few minutes and use a Mind Map to review what you have learnt at the end of a day. Then review it at the end of a week, again at the end of a month, and finally a week before the exams. That way you'll ride your memory wave all the way to your exam – and beyond!

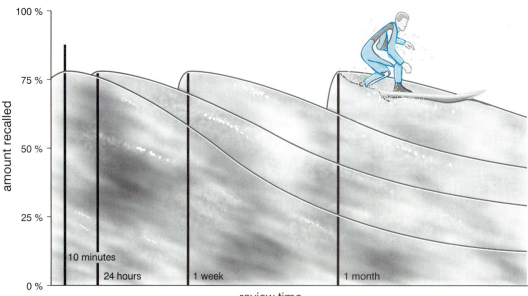

Amazing as your memory is (think of everything you actually *do* have stored in your brain at this moment) the principles on which it operates are very simple: your brain will remember if it (a) has an image (a picture or a symbol); (b) has that image fixed and (c) can link that image to something else.

3 The Mind Map® – a picture of the way you think

Do you *like* taking notes and making vocabulary lists? More importantly, do you like having to go back over and learn them before exams? Most students I know certainly do not! And how do you take your notes and make your lists? Most people take notes and make lists on lined paper, using blue or black ink. The result, visually, is *boring*! And what does your brain do when it is bored? It turns off, tunes out, and goes to sleep! Add a dash of colour, rhythm, imagination, and the whole process becomes much more fun, uses more of your brain's abilities, *and* improves your recall and understanding.

A Mind Map mirrors the way your brain works. It can be used for note-taking and gathering vocabulary phrases and language structures from books or in class, for reviewing what you have just studied, for revising, and for essay planning for coursework and in exams.

It uses all your memory's natural techniques to build up your rapidly growing 'memory muscle'.

You will find Mind Maps throughout this book. Study them, add some colour, personalise them, and then have a go at drawing your own – you'll remember them far better! Put them on your walls and in your files for a quick-and-easy review of the topic.

How to draw a Mind Map

❶ Start in the middle of the page with the page turned sideways. This gives your brain the maximum room for its thoughts.

❷ Always start by drawing a small picture or symbol. Why? Because a picture is worth a thousand words to your brain. And try to use at least three colours, as colour helps your memory even more.

❸ Let your thoughts flow, and write or draw your ideas on coloured branching lines connected to your central image. These key symbols and words are the headings for your topic. The Mind Map at the top of the next page shows you how to start.

❹ Then add facts, further items and ideas, time markers and tenses by drawing more, smaller, branches on to the appropriate main branches, just like a tree.

❺ Always print your word clearly on its line. Use only one word per line. The Mind Map at the foot of the next page shows you how to do this.

❻ To link ideas and thoughts on different branches, use arrows, colours, underlining, and boxes.

How to read a Mind Map

❶ Begin in the centre, the focus of your topic.

❷ The words/images attached to the centre are like chapter headings: read them next.

❸ Always read out from the centre, in every direction (even on the left-hand side, where you will have to read from right to left, instead of the usual left to right).

Using Mind Maps

Mind Maps are a versatile tool – use them for taking notes in class or from books, for solving problems, for brainstorming with friends, and for reviewing and revising for exams – their uses are endless! You will find them invaluable for planning essays for coursework and exams. Number your main branches in the order in which you want to use them and off you go – the main headings for your essay are done and all your ideas are logically organised!

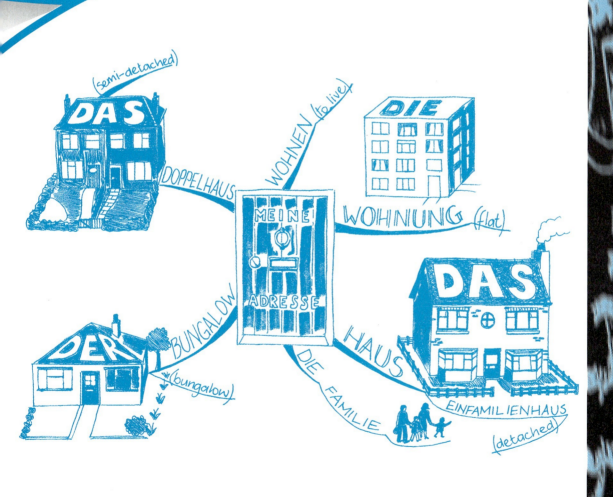

4 Super speed reading

It seems incredible, but it's been proved – the faster you read, the more you understand and remember! So here are some tips to help you to practise reading faster – you'll cover the ground more quickly, remember more, *and* have more time for revision!

★ Read the whole text (whether it's a lengthy book, a long passage or an exam paper) very quickly first, to give your brain an overall idea of what's ahead and get it working. (It's like sending out a scout to look at the territory you have to cover – it's much easier when you know what to expect!) Then read the text again for more detailed information.

★ Have the text a reasonable distance away from your eyes. In this way your eye/brain system will be able to see more at a glance, and will naturally begin to read faster.

★ Take in groups of words at a time. Rather than reading 'slowly and carefully' read faster, more enthusiastically. Your comprehension will rocket!

★ Take in phrases rather than single words while you read.

★ Use a guide. Your eyes are designed to follow movement, so a thin pencil underneath the lines you are reading, moved smoothly along, will 'pull' your eyes to faster speeds.

5 Helpful hints for exam revision

Start to revise at the beginning of the course. Cram at the start, not the end and avoid 'exam panic'!

Use Mind Maps throughout your course, and build a Master Mind Map for each subject – a giant Mind Map that summarises everything you know about the subject.

Use memory techniques such as mnemonics (verses or systems for remembering things like dates and events, or lists).

Get together with one or two friends to revise, compare Mind Maps, and discuss topics.

And finally...

★ *Have fun while you learn* – studies show that those people who enjoy what they are doing understand and remember it more, and generally do it better.

★ *Use your teachers* as resource centres. Ask them for help with specific topics and with more general advice on how you can improve your all-round performance.

★ *Personalise your Revision Guide* by underlining and highlighting, by adding notes and pictures. Allow your brain to have a conversation with it!

Your brain is an amazing piece of equipment – learn to use it, and you, like thousands of students before you will be able to master German with ease. The more you understand and use your brain, the more it will repay you!

Essential starting points

How do I use this book?

This German Revision Guide has eight topic chapters. Each topic covers both Foundation and Higher level material. A numbered checklist at the beginning of each chapter lists the things you should know for each tier within that topic. Use the checklist by shading in the **Kein Problem!** or **Hilfe!** buttons as you work through your revision to keep a record of your progress and to identify where you need to concentrate your efforts. You will also see how your memory and skills are growing.

The chapters contain all the vocabulary and structures that you need to achieve good GCSE grades for any of the exam boards. The language is presented in a way that is easy to follow and remember.

Find out from the start which tiers you have been entered for so that you can see whether to revise the Higher material as well. For example, if you were entered for all the Higher papers except in Writing, you would work through all the Test yourself tasks – leaving out those marked with

Meet the Grün and Müller families

As you work through the chapters you will meet the members of these two families, who are neighbours, and some of their friends. These characters are there to help you revise your German; they have prepared written and spoken items about themselves and their lives – descriptions, drawings, letters and conversations. Make use of the practice exercises based on their activities.

Use the checklist and the Wortautomat

Work through each chapter at your own pace: shade in the checklist (**Kein Problem!** / **Hilfe!**). For all of the items that you have shaded or ticked on the **Hilfe!** button, go on to read the **Wortautomat** looking out for that particular point. In this way, you will be able to make the most of your revision time.

Then move on to the Test yourself tasks which include exercises in the four skills areas (Listening, Speaking, Reading, Writing);

these will help you to recall the content of the chapter and to give you some exam practice. Remember: always mark your answers using the upside-down key. If your answer is not satisfactory, look back at the **Wortautomat** for the particular points that have troubled you.

Before moving on from one chapter to the next, you should look back at the checklist to be certain that you are confident with all of the items on the list. You should have shaded all the **Kein Problem!** buttons before you move on.

Putting it all together

Chapter 9 lists some of the frequently used exam question instructions. Make a point of learning these so that you understand what's required to answer the question in the exam (e.g. tick the box): take every opportunity to show the examiner all your hard-earned knowledge! If you do not understand the instructions you will not do yourself justice.

Most of the instructions on your exam papers will be in German.

This section also explains the five *Areas of Experience* that make up your GCSE

German Revision Guide

syllabus; these are displayed in Mind Map form for easy comprehension.

Make the most of the Mind Maps

The topics covered in the eight chapters are linked to the memory jogging Mind Maps in Chapter 10 (pages 99 – 124); these connect the ideas and vocabulary in the chapters to help you learn the vital vocabulary. Here are some more characters to help you through your revision: the WHAT memory jogger, the HOW memory jogger, the WHERE memory jogger, the WHO memory jogger and the WHICH memory jogger. This section is designed to suggest ways of using Mind Maps and pictures to create your own personal German fitness programme.

provide a useful reference to which you can refer while working through your *Revision Guide*.

Mock exam

Chapter 12 is a practice mock exam. There are exam questions for Listening, Speaking, Reading and Writing. Work through the tier which you intend to tackle in the exam for each exam part. Time yourself on the individual questions and mark your work afterwards – re-revise the elements that let you down.

> **Please write on me!**
>
> Make notes as you go, use highlighter pens, and make your own Mind Maps. This is one book on which you can make your 'mark'! Feel free to make notes to yourself in the book. Keep blank paper and coloured pens by you as you revise in case you feel an urge to Mind Map! Revising should be an 'active' use of time so that you remember more effectively!

Grammar: last but not least

Take the opportunity of getting to grips with German grammar with Frau Grün in Chapter 11. All the terms are fully explained as if they are items in Frau Grün's store cupboard, with examples using vocabulary already covered in the topic chapters (chapters 1 – 8), Mind Maps and pictures to help you remember. The grammar rules are explained in plain English so that you can understand and use them yourself – without making any mistakes!

German verbs are easy once you've worked through this section. There are also some helpful hints on using dictionaries and neat memory boosting ideas for grammar.

At the end of this section there are some more characters for you to meet: this time of the canine variety! You will find the grammar explanations

Train your memory

Your memory improves the more you use it – according to scientific research! Read through the pages 5 – 8 again. Realise that you cannot leave all of that German revision until the night before your exam – there just won't be enough time!

Plan out the time before your German exam so that you revise a little every day allowing your mind to absorb the information. Give more time to the topics that you find most difficult. Bear in mind the other subjects you are taking and juggle your revision time carefully.

Some people find that they are most receptive to learning and memorising in the mornings, but only you can decide what works best for you. Be aware of what are the hardest topics and structures for you, and don't leave them to the last minute!

Learning and revising skills

TEN TOP TIPS for learning vocabulary

1. Use different coloured pens to highlight masculine, feminine, and neuter words on Mind Maps.
2. Draw an item or symbol for key vocabulary.
3. Don't try to learn more than ten words at a time.
4. Take ten minutes to make a Mind Map. Then, after a break, take another ten minutes to write out the vocabulary using the Mind Map.
5. Use a list of ten words, start at the bottom and work upwards, as well as downwards.
6. Visualise each item of vocabulary as you say the word in German.
7. Record yourself – play it back and imagine the item again.
8. Ask friends, brothers, sisters or parents to test you on vocabulary.
9. Remember that with regular effort you can build a bigger vocabulary and recall it.
10. Think positive. Vocabulary is the key and the more often you learn small chunks, the easier it gets.

HEATING   If you are too warm while you are revising, you might find that you start falling asleep – not ideal for training your memory! Fresh air helps concentration so open the windows while you are working, or at least during your short breaks.

SPACE   Organise your desk or table so that your books, notes, dictionaries, pens and paper are within easy reach. If you have to keep getting up to look for things you will be easily distracted.

POSITION   Make sure your chair is at the right height and keeping your back straight while your are revising. You might get back-ache if you sit awkwardly. Never work in an armchair or lying on your bed: you will be too relaxed to take much in!

FUEL   Meals are very important. Pay as much attention to your food intake as does an athlete training for a competition! Limit the amount of sugary and fatty things you eat as these increase irritability and can disrupt concentration. Likewise, stimulating drinks (such as coffee and tea) can revive you in the short term, but they might also disturb your sleep pattern and affect your memory if you're tired.

Are you sitting comfortably?

You need to be at ease when you are revising. Here are some tips to help you choose an ideal working environment.

LOCATION   Never revise in the kitchen or the living room with the TV on or with brothers or sisters around. Find a place that is quiet and where there are no distractions. If you find it hard to revise at home, you could go to your library.

LIGHTING   Natural light is best. If you can, sit by a window. If you have to work in artificial light, try to use a lamp rather than fluorescent lighting as this can give you eye strain. Avoid shadows; make sure that the light comes from your left if you are right-handed, and from your right if you are left-handed.

Which exams will I be taking?

For your GCSE German exam, if you are following a MEG, NEAB, EDEXCEL (formerly ULEAC) or WJEC course, you will be assessed on four areas of language skills: Listening, Speaking, Reading and Writing. You will either sit an exam for each of these skills or you will do a coursework option (see below).

Which tier: Foundation or Higher?

You can take the different exam parts at either the Foundation or Higher tier. This gives you the following three options:

- You take exams in all four language skills at the Foundation tier (possible grades G - C)
- You take exams in all four language skills at the Higher tier (possible grades D - A*)
- You 'mix and match'. This is a mixture of tiers for the different exam parts (Listening, Speaking, Reading, Writing), according to your strengths and weaknesses. This might limit your grades.

What grades can I get if I mix tiers?

A Foundation tier paper equals a possible total of up to 5 points – e.g. C = 5 points.

A Higher tier paper equals a possible total of up to 8 points (but you *must* score at least 3 points on a Higher tier paper or you will get zero points!).

If you do the coursework option, up to 8 points will be available depending on the difficulty of the task and on how well you do!

Your total number of points for the four different skills areas will be added together to give an overall points score out of 32. The points are then converted to a final grade.

G = 2 - 5 points
G = 6 - 9 points
E = 10 - 13 points
D = 14 - 17 points
C = 18 - 21 points
B = 22 - 25 points
A = 26 - 29 points
A* = 30 - 32 points

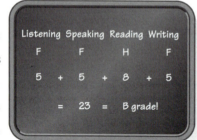

So, if you were to do three Foundation tier papers (3 × 5 possible points) and one Higher tier paper (1 × 8 possible points = total 23 points) the highest grade you could possible be awarded would be a B.

> Remember! Make sure you know which tier you are doing for which paper before you start revising and before the exam, and check the tier on your exam paper on the day. You can only do one tier for each paper, so check that it is the correct one!

What is the coursework option?

- **Writing** Most exam boards offer the Writing coursework option which means that you can build up a file of written work during Years 10 and 11; usually, three pieces of work are submitted to the board.

Find out from you teacher if you will be doing the coursework option. If you are, you will receive lots of guidance. You will be told which subjects to write about, how much you have to write (this will vary from 40 – 150 words usually depending on the type of task and the final grade you are aiming for). Your teacher will mark this work initially, so you will have a good idea of how well your are progressing.

There are lots of writing tasks in this book; these will help you to practise for your coursework tasks. One piece of work, at least, will have to be done in class in 'controlled conditions'. You will still be able to use dictionaries and reference materials, but you won't get any help from people in the classroom.

- **Speaking** EDEXCEL (formerly ULEAC) offers a Speaking coursework option. If you do this you will build up evidence of your performance on cassette during Years 10 and 11. You will be expected to perform both role play and conversation tasks. Ask your teacher for further details.

You cannot do both Writing and Speaking coursework options.

What happens with a SEG Modular course?

If you are following a SEG Modular course, you will be assessed both during the course in Years 10 and 11 and at the end of your course in Year 11.

The SEG syllabus requires you to work through four modules of work as follows:

Module 1 tests Listening, Speaking and Reading through coursework (February, Year 10) and concentrates on these topics: Personal Details, Family and Pets, Home and Local Environment, Local and Leisure Environment, Health and School.

Module 2 tests Listening and Reading through an end-of-Module test (June, Year 10) and concentrates on these topics: Tourist Information, Travel by Bus, Directions, Money and Banks, Shopping, Food and Drink, Entertainment, Emergencies.

Module 3 (February, Year 11) tests Speaking and Reading through coursework and concentrates on Holidays and Accommodation, Travel and Transport, Bank, Services, Weather, Directions, Shopping.

Module 4 tests Listening, Speaking, Reading and Writing through exam (Year 22, June) and concentrates on Personal Identity and Relationships, the Environment, School, Future Plans, Work, Spending Money and Health.

Remember! The topics covered in the modules feature in this book – work through them in the order you meet the topics in your modules 1 – 4.

During the exam

- Structure your time so that you have enough time to answer all of the questions. Don't spend too long on one question. First answer the questions you can do easily and then go back to the more difficult ones.
- Answer all the questions.
- Look carefully at the number of marks you can get for each question. For example, three marks means you must give three items of information in your answer.
- Stick to the point. Give opinions and reasons wherever you can and use the different tenses where appropriate. Don't pad out your answer with irrelevant material, it will be obvious that you can't answer the question.
- Plan your answers, especially for the Writing paper. Draw a quick Mind Map.
- Write clearly. Ask for some blank sheets of paper if you want to write out notes or plan with Mind Maps. Remember to cross out neatly any work that you don't want the examiner to mark.
- Leave some time at the end to look over your answers as a final check.
- Remember to answer in the correct language.

USING A DICTIONARY IN THE EXAM
You can use a bilingual dictionary during Reading and Writing exams, and some boards (e.g. NEAB and WJEC) also allow you to use a dictionary before and after the cassette is played in the Listening exam. All boards allow you to use a dictionary while preparing your Speaking exam, but not during the actual exam (See notes on pages 128 and 135). Here are some key points to remember:

TAKE CARE   Make sure that when you are looking up a German word (e.g. what's the German word for 'a bicycle') you look in the English-German section for 'bicycle', and then read off the German translation. If you are looking up the English meaning of a German word (e.g. 'Rad'), make sure you look in the German-English section to read off the English (e.g. wheel); then to double-check what you have found, you should look up the word in the English-German section to make sure that the word you have found is appropriate in the context (e.g. is it 'wheel' or 'bicycle'?).

TIME SAVING   Using a dictionary takes (and can waste) valuable time in an exam. Use one only when it is absolutely necessary. Do not look up every single word you don't know in a long Reading text – you might not need to know every word! But, do use a dictionary to check the meaning of words in questions if you are unsure.

SPEED   Practise using a dictionary so that you can build up your 'search speed'. If possible use the same edition that you will be using in the exam. This will mean you waste less time and that you'll feel more confident about how to use one well. Make sure that you know what the abbreviations mean.

DON'T PANIC   Learn as much vocabulary as you can before the exam but remember you will probably not know every word in the exam – so don't panic!

LAST RESORT   Work through as much of each exercise as you can without using a dictionary. It is there to help you in an emergency only.

German Revision Guide

Last minute tips!

If you write in the wrong language you will not get any marks, cruel though that may sound! For Reading and Listening exams, up to one-fifth of the marks might be awarded to questions which have English instructions or require answers written in English. Remember, if the instructions are in *English* you have to write out an answer in *English*; if the instructions are in *German* you have to write out an answer in *German*.

LISTENING

- If you can use a dictionary before the exam (NEAB, WJEC) read through the questions quickly, and look up words you're not sure about. Use the time at the end to check for words you need to write in the answers.
- Remember that you don't need to write in full sentences.
- Look carefully at the pictures in the questions.
- If you miss a question, don't panic, keep listening, you can have another 'go' in the second listen through!
- Write in the correct language!
- Don't agonise over a spelling: provided your *message is clear* examiners will tolerate small mistakes!

SPEAKING

- Don't panic! Your teacher is there to help and is probably as nervous as you are about performing well!
- Remember your cue card if you are doing a presentation and arrive five minutes early.
- Use the preparation time well, use a dictionary to look up items shown in visual cues or the role plays.
- Read the English settings – they are there to explain the situation, to put you at ease and to help you!
- Try to spot the 'unexpected element' in the second Foundation Level, or the first Higher Level role play.
- While preparing, think what the examiner's lead-in question might be if you have a cue which says '**Wie antworten Sie**?', and how you could answer.
- If you don't understand a question or want something repeated, say so – Ich verstehe nicht. Bitte wiederholen Sie. This will give you a few seconds and keeps the German flowing!

- Remember: to get a C grade you need to use past, present and future tenses. Learn thoroughly a few of the phrases in this book in each of these tenses on each topic.
- Smile as you go in, it will relax you!
- Remember to work out exactly where you went on holiday last year, what you did last weekend, last night, this morning (past tense) and what you will do tonight, this weekend, in the summer, next year (future tense). Try not to fish around for ideas in the exam room – have your ideas 'straight' before you go in so that you only have to recall the appropriate phrases in German.

READING

- Do not use a dictionary to look up every word you don't know.
- Read through the text and questions once before you even attempt to answer any questions or use the dictionary.
- Check that you understand the instructions.
- Examiners are checking that you have understood. They will not deduct marks for incorrect spellings. But your message should be clear to gain marks.
- Try not to leave gaps – make an intelligent guess rather than leave a gap! You don't have to write in full sentences but the *message should be clear*.

WRITING

- Read the question at least twice before you start.
- Check the instructions.
- Use a dictionary to check the meanings of words in the question if you are at all unsure.
- Plan your answer using a Mind Map so that you cover all the communication points.
- On longer answers, examiners will look for accurate German, so check spellings and tenses very carefully.
- Don't use the dictionary to 'experiment with new phrases' – stick to what you know and can say well.

If your exam is tomorrow, take a break and have a long bath! You could flick through chapter 10 of this book – the memory jogging Mind Maps – for 20 minutes and then have a rest. Let your mind relax before the big day! *Viel Glück!*

1

All about Marlene

If you're feeling a bit rusty, don't panic, because now it's time to meet someone who wants to help you. She's a little odd, but deep down she's a really nice person.

What to do...

- Read Marlene's interview, which starts below.
- Use the **Wortautomat** on the next page to help you understand everything she says (including the bits in the box).

 • Change the words in *bold italics* to write an interview about yourself. This time, ignore the boxed bit.

 • Change the words in *bold italics* to write an interview about yourself, including the boxed bit.

Hallo! Wie heißt du?
Ich heiße **Marlene** und ich bin **sechzehn** Jahre alt. Mein Geburtstag ist am **29. Februar**. Ich bin **Deutsche** und ich komme aus **Kippenstadt**.

He Leute!

checklist

What would you say if you had to ...

talk about yourself, family, friends and pets?

understand about other people?

spell out your name, street, and town?

talk and understand about hobbies and interests?

say how you feel about others?

give opinions about hobbies and interests?

German Revision Guide

Was machst du gern?
Ich *schlafe* gern und *höre* gern *sehr laute Musik*!
Ich *gehe* nicht gern *in die Schule* – das ist sehr langweilig.

Wie siehst du aus, Marlene?
Ich bin *sehr groß* und *schlank*. Ich habe *kurze, glatte, rote* Haare und *grüne* Augen. Normalerweise trage ich *große Ohrringe, schwarze Jeans* und *ein altes T-Shirt*.

Was für eine Person bist du?
Ich bin *sehr intelligent* und *gut gelaunt*.

Hast du Geschwister?
Ja, ich habe *einen kleinen Bruder aber keine Schwester. Mein Bruder heißt Martin*.

Und Haustiere?
Ja. Wir haben *drei große Hunde, vierzehn Katzen und eine Tarantel*.

> **HIGHER** **Wie verstehst du dich mit deiner Familie?**
> Ich verstehe mich *gut* mit meiner Familie, denn meine Eltern sind *sehr lustig und sympathisch*, und mein kleiner Bruder ist *wirklich süß*. Aber wir verstehen uns nicht sehr gut mit den Nachbarn...

Was sind deine Hobbys?
Meine Hobbys sind
  Fußball spielen,
  Tanzen,
  Rad fahren,
  Reiten,
  Schwimmen,
  Musik hören,
  Malen,
  Lesen,
  Briefe schreiben,
  Briefmarken sammeln.

What are your hobbies?
My hobbies are
  playing football,
  dancing,
  cycling,
  riding,
  swimming,
  listening to music,
  painting,
  reading,
  writing letters,
  collecting stamps.

Was machst du (nicht) gern?
Ich höre (nicht) gern

  Musik.
  Popmusik.
  klassische Musik.

Ich sehe (nicht) gern fern.

Ich lese (nicht) gern
  Comics.
  Zeitschriften.
  Zeitungen.
  Romane.
  Krimis.
  Horrorgeschichten.
  Science-Fiction Geschichten.
  Liebesgeschichten.

Ich spiele (nicht) gern
  Fußball.
  Tennis.
  Federball.
  Karten.
  Gitarre.
  Klavier.

What do you (not) like doing?
I (don't) like
  listening to
    music.
    pop music.
    classical music.

I (don't) like watching TV.

I (don't) like reading
  comics.
  magazines.
  newspapers.
  novels.
  thrillers.
  horror stories.
  sci-fi stories.

  love stories.

I (don't) like playing
  football.
  tennis.
  badminton.
  cards.
  guitar.
  piano.

Wortautomat

Wie alt bist du?
Ich bin fünfzehn.
         sechzehn.

Wann hast du Geburtstag?
Am... (➔See page 101 for dates.)

Woher kommst du?

Ich komme aus...
Ich bin Engländer /
         Engländerin.
         Schotte /
         Schottin.
         Waliser /
         Waliserin.
         Irländer /
         Irländerin.

How old are you?
I'm fifteen.
    sixteen.

When's your birthday?
On...

Where do you come from?

I come from...
I'm English.

         Scottish.

         Welsh.

         Irish.

Geige	violin.	**Hast du Geschwister?**	**Have you got any brothers or sisters?**
Flöte	flute.		
Ich gehe (nicht) gern	I (don't) like going to	Ja, ich habe	Yes, I've got
in den Park.	the park.	einen Bruder	a brother
in die Disco.	disco.	zwei Brüder	two brothers
in die Stadt.	town.	eine Schwester	a sister
ins Kino.	cinema.	zwei Schwestern	two sisters
ins Theater.	theatre.	aber keinen Bruder.	but no brothers.
		keine Schwester.	no sisters.
Wie siehst du aus?	**What do you look like?**	Ich bin Einzelkind.	I'm an only child.
Ich bin	I'm		
ziemlich klein.	quite small.	**Hast du Haustiere?**	**Have you got any pets?**
sehr groß.	very tall.	Ich habe	I've got
schlank /	slim / thin.	einen Hund.	a dog.
dünn.		zwei Hunde.	two dogs.
dick.	fat.	eine Katze.	a cat.
		zwei Katzen.	two cats.
Ich habe	I have	ein / zwei Kaninchen.	one / two rabbits.
kurze Haare.	short hair.	ein / zwei	one / two guinea-pigs.
lange	long	Meerschweinchen.	
glatte	straight	viele Fische.	lots of fish.
lockige	curly		
rote	red		
(dunkel)braune	(dark) brown		
(hell)blonde	(light) blond		
schwarze	black		

Ich habe	I have
braune Augen.	brown eyes.
grüne	green
blaue	blue
graue	grey
Ich trage eine Brille.	I wear glasses.
Was für eine Person bist du?	**What sort of person are you?**
Ich bin	I'm
(ziemlich) fleißig.	(quite) hardworking.
(sehr) faul.	(very) lazy.
intelligent.	intelligent.
freundlich.	friendly.
lustig.	funny.
laut.	loud.
schüchtern.	shy.
sympathisch.	pleasant.
nett.	nice.
großzügig.	generous.
unternehmungslustig.	adventurous.

German Revision Guide

Was machst du lieber?	**What do you prefer to do?**
Ich höre lieber Popmusik.	I prefer listening to pop music.
Ich lese Comics.	reading comics.
Ich spiele Tennis.	playing tennis.
Ich gehe in die Stadt.	going into town.
Am liebsten höre ich Rapmusik.	Best of all I like to listen to rap.
lese ich Zeitungen.	read newspapers.
spiele ich Fußball.	play football.
gehe ich schwimmen.	go swimming.
Wofür interessierst du dich?	**What are you interested in?**
Ich interessiere mich für Musik.	I'm interested in music.
Sport.	sport.
Ich bin Mitglied in einem Sportverein.	I'm a member of a sports club.
einer Hockeymannschaft.	a hockey team.
Was trägst du normalerweise?	**What do you usually wear?**
Normalerweise trage ich (große) Ohrringe	Usually I wear (big) ear-rings.
Meistens einen schwarzen Minirock.	Mostly a black miniskirt.
eine blaue Jacke.	a blue jacket.
ein rotes Hemd.	a red shirt.
(➜*See page 113 for clothes.*)	
Wie heißen deine Geschwister?	**What are your brothers and sisters called?**
Ich habe einen Bruder, der Michael heißt.	I've got a brother called Michael.
Ich habe eine Schwester, die Vicki heißt.	I've got a sister called Vicki.
Wie verstehst du dich mit deiner Familie?	**How do you get on with your family?**
Ich verstehe mich gut/nicht (besonders) gut mit meiner Familie, denn…	I get on well/not (particularly) well with my family, because…

Have you understood everything Marlene has said? And have you changed the interview so that it's about you?

When you've done that, you will need to memorise your answer. Marlene, who is very clever, might be able to help. She sometimes finds it hard to remember what she has said in the past. So she draws pictures or symbols, together with key words, of the phrases she wants to remember. She knows that pictures stick in her mind much better than words on their own.

He Leute!

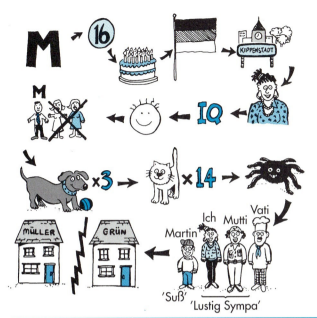

Here are Marlene's symbols for her interview:

Once she has drawn the symbols, she looks at each one and repeats the phrase that goes with it until she is confident that she can remember both symbol and phrase without looking.

Why not try Marlene's technique? If you're already fairly confident, you could use key words (name, age, etc.) instead of symbols to jog your memory.

Spell names / addresses

You will need to understand, as well as say, the German alphabet. Listen to the alphabet on the cassette and write down which other letters rhyme with...

a, h —

b, c — — — — — —

q —

Which ones sound almost the same as English letters?

f — — — — —

Which ones are left? Listen again carefully and match up the letters with the correct pronunciation below.

i	'yot'	x	'tset'
j	'airr'	y	'icks'
r	'fow'	z	'üpsilon'
v	'ee'		

There are a few letters in German that you don't have in English:

- **ß** is 'ess-tset', and is like a double *s*.
- **ä** is 'ay', as in *pay*.
- **ö** is 'ur', as in *blur*.
- **ü** is made by holding your lips as if you're going to say 'ooh', but saying 'ee'. Try it!

The two little dots over **ä**, **ö** and **ü** are called an umlaut.

Draw a picture to help you remember each letter. Try to get the shape of the letter into the picture.

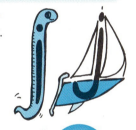

Practice

Time yourself. How quickly can you do the following?

Spell out your full name / your street name / your town / the first names of ten people you know.

With a friend, take it in turns to spell out words / names / towns as quickly as you can. Without writing anything, the other person has to work out what has been spelt.

Answers

Alphabet:
a, h: **k**.
b, c: **d, e, g, p, t, w**.
q: **u**.
f, l, m, n, o, s.
i = 'ee'; j = 'yot'; r = 'airr'; v = 'fow'; x = 'icks';
y = 'üpsilon'; z = 'tset'.

German Revision Guide

You will also need to know the following phrases, which both mean *How do you spell that?*

Wie schreibt man das?

Wie buchstabiert man das?

Neighbours from hell

But Marlene is getting impatient. Now that she's told you about herself, she's dying to have a good gossip about the people next door.

 Meine Nachbarn sind immer schlecht gelaunt! Die Mutter ist sehr streng, und die Kinder sind langweilig.

Die Tochter ist neun Jahre alt. Sie heißt Gretchen und ihr Geburtstag ist am 1. Juni. Sie ist klein und hat lange blonde Haare und blaue Augen. Sie liest gern Liebesgeschichten und geht gern reiten. Ich finde sie schrecklich!

Der Sohn ist fünfzehn. Er heißt Gerhard. Sein Geburtstag ist am 25. August. Er spielt gern Geige und hört gern klassische Musik. Das finde ich doof! Er ist kleiner als ich und hat schwarze Haare und braune Augen.

Gerhard sieht ziemlich gut aus. Ich verstehe mich nicht gut mit ihm, denn ich kann ihn nicht leiden!

Marlene would like to know about the people in your life. Using the **Wortautomat** below, change what she says so that you can talk about your family and friends.

(Remember, if you're doing Foundation Level, you need to understand the bits in the Higher box but you don't need to use them yourself. But if you're doing Higher Level, you need to use the bits in the Higher box .)

Wortautomat

Wie heißt er / sie? Was macht er / sie gern?		What's his / her name? What does he / she like doing?	
Meine Mutter	heißt …	My mum	is called…
Mein Vater	ist …	My dad	is…
Mein Bruder	hat …	My brother	has…
Meine Schwester	liest gern.	My sister	likes reading.
Mein (bester) Freund	geht gern schwimmen.	My (best) friend (*male*)	likes swimming.
Meine (beste) Freundin	spielt gern Gitarre.	My (best) friend (*female*)	likes playing the guitar.
Er / Sie	hört gern Popmusik.	He / She	likes listening to pop music.

Wie heißen sie? Was machen sie gern?		What are they called? What do they like doing?
Meine Eltern	heißen…	My parents are called…
Meine Brüder	sind…	My brothers are…
Meine Schwestern	haben…	My sisters have…

He Leute!

Sie	lesen gern.		They like reading.
	gehen gern kegeln.		going bowling.
	spielen gern Fußball.		playing football.
	hören gern Radio.		listening to music.

Wann hat er / sie Geburtstag? — **When's his / her birthday?**
Sein / Ihr Geburtstag ist am… — His / Her birthday's on…

Wie sieht er / sie aus? — **What does he / she look like?**
Wie sehen sie aus? — **What do they look like?**

Er / Sie ist	hübsch.	He / She is	pretty / good-looking.
Sie sind	hässlich.	They are	ugly.
	interessant.		interesting.
	langweilig.		boring.
	(zu) streng.		(too) strict.
manchmal	gut gelaunt.	sometimes	good-tempered
oft	schlecht gelaunt.	often	bad-tempered.
immer	böse.	always	angry.

Er hat einen Bart. — He has a beard.
einen Schnurrbart. — a moustache.

Er / Sie ist	kleiner	als ich.	He / She is	smaller	than me.
	größer	mein Bruder.		taller	my brother.
	dicker	meine Schwester.		fatter	my sister.
	schlanker			slimmer	
	intelligenter			more intelligent	
	fleißiger			harder working	

Wie findest du ihn / sie? — **What do you think of him / her?**
Ich finde ihn schrecklich. — I think he's terrible.
sie toll. — she's great.

Sieht er / sie gut aus? — **Is he / she good-looking?**
Er / Sie sieht gut aus. — He / She is good-looking.
nicht besonders gut — isn't particularly

Wie verstehst du dich mit…? — **How well do you get on with…?**
Ich verstehe mich gut mit ihm. — I get on well with him.
nicht gut meinem Bruder, — I don't get on with my brother,
ihr, — her,
meiner Schwester, — my sister,
ihnen, — them,
meinen Eltern, — my parents,
denn er / sie ist… — because he / she is…
sie sind… — they are…
ich kann ihn nicht leiden. — I can't stand him.
sie — her.

When you are happy with what you've written about your family and friends, memorise it using the same technique as before.

Creature comforts

One of the reasons that Marlene doesn't get on with her neighbours is that Gerhard and Gretchen don't share her love of spiders. Marlene can't understand how anyone could object to Haarig – her beautiful, black tarantula!

Meine Tarantel heißt Haarig, weil sie sehr haarig ist. Sie ist zwei Jahre alt, hat lange haarige Beine, und ist schön, schwarz und sehr, sehr groß. Sie ist wirklich süß und intelligent und ich liebe sie!

Tell Marlene about your pets (names, ages, appearance, character). You can use many of the phrases you've already practised, so there's not much more to learn for this bit. Remember to check the gender of your pet before you start. This is not the same as its sex! You may be surprised to find that in German **Hund** is masculine, so you must call your dog **er**, even though her name is Bess; **Katze** is feminine, so your cat is a **sie**; and **Kaninchen** is neuter, so your rabbit is an **es**.

You'll find some more help in the **Wortautomat**.

Now memorise the description of your pet.

You have now revised how to speak and write about yourself, your friends and family, and your pets. You also know how to spell out your name, street and town in German, and you can understand other people doing the same. There's one more thing to do before you try the **Test Yourself** tasks at the end of this unit: learn to recognise some words which you probably wouldn't use yourself, but will need to understand for the Reading and Listening tests.

Wortautomat

Wie heißt dein Haustier?
Mein Hund
Meine Katze
Mein Kaninchen heißt…
Meine Fische heißen…

weil
  sie sehr haarig ist.
  er braun
  es klein
  sie schön sind.

What's your pet called?
My dog's
My cat's
My rabbit's called…
My fish are called…

because
  he / she's very hairy.
  brown.
  small
  they're beautiful.

Welche Farbe hat er / sie / es?
Wie ist er / sie / es?

Er ist schwarz.
Sie gelb.
Es weiß.
Sie sind grün.
  grau.
  rot.
  orange.
  blau.
  lila.
  süß.
  unartig.

What colour is he / she?
What does he / she look like?

He / She's black.
  yellow.
  white.
They're green.
  grey.
  red.
  orange.
  blue.
  purple.
  sweet.
  naughty.

Wie findest du dein Tier?
Ich liebe ihn.
  sie.
  es.
  sie.

What do you think of your pet?
I love him / her.
  them.

Martin's magnetic charm

Unfortunately for you, Marlene's little brother Martin has got hold of the word list and mixed up the English translations, so you will have to sort them out before you learn them...

Pair up the German with its English translation.

allein	married
das Alter	twin
die Geburt	birth
geboren	happy
feiern	born
das Land	to sign
die Dame	poor
das Kind	post-code
das Mädchen	alone
der Mann	girl
der Onkel	uncle
die Tante	road / street
der Zwilling	aunt
arm	rich
glücklich	(gentle)man
ledig	lady
reich	age
verheiratet	to celebrate
die Postleitzahl	dialling code
die Staatsangehörigkeit	signature
die Straße (Str.)	grandparents
unterschreiben	where you live
die Unterschrift	nationality
die Vorwahl	adult
der Wohnort	budgerigar
der Erwachsene	single
die Großeltern	country
der Herr	man
der Wellensittich	child

Now check your answers. Underline any you got wrong and write out the German and English correctly. Try doing the same exercise again, but this time only include the words you got wrong the first time. (You will have to mix up the English words yourself.)

Sorting out words is a good way to learn them, so you should be able to recognise most of the words in the list by now. So that you remember them, practise saying the more difficult ones aloud and link the sound of the word with a picture either in your mind or on paper.

Test yourself

Task 1

Eine Kassette von einem neuen Brieffreund.

Bitte ausfüllen:

Name:	....
Alter:	....
Wohnort:	....
Geschwister:	....
Hobbys:	....
Haustiere:	....

Answers: word list

allein – alone
das Alter – age
die Geburt – birth
geboren – born
feiern – to celebrate
das Land – country
die Dame – lady
das Kind – child
das Mädchen – girl
der Mann – man
der Onkel – uncle
die Tante – aunt
der Zwilling – twin
arm – poor
glücklich – happy
ledig – single
reich – rich
verheiratet – married
die Postleitzahl – post-code
die Staatsangehörigkeit – nationality
die Straße (Str.) – road / street
unterschreiben – to sign
die Unterschrift – signature
die Vorwahl – dialling code
der Wohnort – where you live
der Erwachsene – adult
die Großeltern – grandparents
der Herr – (gentle)man
der Wellensittich – budgerigar

German Revision Guide

Task 1 Answers
Name: Klaus Zimmermann; **Alter:** 16; **Wohnort:** Gaggenau; **Geschwister:** keine; **Hobbys:** Fußball, Kegeln; **Haustiere:** zwei Hunde.

Task 2

Freizeit: Was macht Anke gern? Was macht Kurt gern? (✓)

Was macht Anke nicht gern? Was macht Kurt nicht gern? (✗)

	📺	🏸	🎵	🏀	HALLO
Kurt					
Anke		—			

Task 2 Answers

Anke	✓	✗	✓	✓	—
Kurt	✗	✓	✓	✓	—
	HALLO	🏀	🎵	🏸	📺

Task 3

Role-play: You are on a boat trip on the Rhine when a German girl comes up to you and says hello. Ask her name, age, where she comes from, whether she has any brothers or sisters and what she likes and dislikes.

name … ?	brothers / sisters … ?
age … ?	pets … ?	likes … ?
where from … ?	dislikes … ?

Task 4

Conversation: How long can you talk about yourself, family, friends and pets? Use your own symbols, or the Mind Map below, as prompts and get a friend to time you. If you have a cassette recorder, record yourself. Then you can listen to yourself just before the Speaking Test to boost your confidence.

> **HIGHER LEVEL** Add feelings about others and opinions about hobbies to the Mind Map.

2

Greenhouse gas

It's Friday afternoon and Gretchen Grün is in her room trying to get her homework out of the way before the weekend. This week's project is entitled **Mein Haus**.

It's been a long week, and Gretchen is tired and can't think what to write. Suddenly she remembers that her teacher dictated a list of useful questions which she keyed into her lap-top computer. There's only one problem: Martin Müller has been messing around with magnets again and has managed to mix up all the words.

Your job is to help Gretchen sort them out. What questions can you make from the jumbled list below?

1. wohnst Wo du ?
2. Addresse Was deine ist ?
3. du in Wohnst einem einer oder Haus in Wohnung ?
4. gibt Zimmer es in deinem Haus Wie viele ?
5. es Zimmer Welche gibt ?
6. dein Wie ist Zimmer groß ?
7. Farbe hat Welche Schlafzimmer dein ?
8. Was deinem es gibt in Zimmer ?
9. Badezimmer ist das Wo ?
10. und einen ihr Garten Habt Garage eine ?

Now that she has the questions, Gretchen is able to write a good description of her house. And as you helped her, she'll let you read what she's written and use it to write about your own home.

Bei uns

checklist

What would you say if you had to …

	Kein Problem!	Hilfe!
FOUNDATION LEVEL		
give your own address?	●	●
talk about your home and say where it is?	●	●
talk and ask about rooms, garage, garden?	●	●
say what jobs you do around the house?	●	●
say how much pocket money you get and how you spend it?	●	●
HIGHER LEVEL		
say whether you have your own room?	●	●
offer and ask for help to do something around the house?	●	●
say what members of the family do to help at home?	●	●
say whether you have enough money, and why?	●	●

German Revision Guide

Meine Adresse ist Bachstraße 25, Kippenstadt, Deutschland, und ich wohne in einem schönen kleinen Haus gegenüber vom Park und neben Martin Müller. (Das ist schrecklich!)

Wir haben einen langen Garten, eine Garage für die Fahrräder und einen Schuppen für Mutti (sie arbeitet gern im Garten). Der Garten gefällt mir sehr gut.

Bei uns gibt es sieben Zimmer: unten, die Küche, das Esszimmer und das Wohnzimmer; oben, drei Schlafzimmer und das Badezimmer.

Mein Schlafzimmer ist mein Lieblingszimmer! Es ist neben dem Badezimmer – sehr praktisch! In meinem Zimmer gibt es ein Bett, einen roten Kleiderschrank, eine weiße Kommode und einen weißen Schreibtisch. Auf dem Schreibtisch ist mein Computer. An der Wand habe ich viele Posters. Die Tapete ist rosa und der Teppich ist grau.

Ich habe mein eigenes Zimmer– das finde ich toll!

 Mein Haus gefällt mir wirklich gut, weil es so modern und gemütlich ist.

Answers

1. Wo wohnst du?
2. Was ist deine Adresse?
3. Wohnst du in einem Haus oder in einer Wohnung?
4. Wie viele Zimmer gibt es in deinem Haus?
5. Welche Zimmer gibt es?
6. Wie groß ist dein Zimmer?
7. Welche Farbe hat dein Zimmer?
8. Was gibt es in deinem Schlafzimmer?
9. Wo ist das Badezimmer?
10. Habt ihr einen Garten und eine Garage?

Wortautomat

Was ist deine Adresse?
Meine Adresse ist..., Großbritannien.

What's your address?
My address is..., Great Britain.

Wohnst du in einem Haus oder in einer Wohnung?
Ich wohne in einem großen Einfamilienhaus.
                kleinen Doppelhaus.
                Reihenhaus.
     einer   Wohnung.

Do you live in a house or a flat?
I live in a big   detached house.
         small semi-detached house.
         terraced house.
         flat.

Wo wohnst du genau?
Ich wohne neben dem   Park.
       gegenüber vom   Supermarkt.
       in der Nähe vom Bahnhof.

Where exactly do you live?
I live next to   the park.
    opposite the supermarket.
    near   the station.

Ich wohne neben der   Bank.
       gegenüber von der   Bushaltestelle.
       in der Nähe von der U-Bahn.

I live next to   the bank.
    opposite the bus-stop.
    near   the underground.

Habt ihr einen Garten?
       eine Garage?
Wir haben einen kleinen Garten vor   dem Haus.
               großen   hinter
       keinen   Garten.
       eine   Garage.
       keine

Have you got a garden?
         a garage?
We have a   small garden in front of the house.
         big   behind
         no   garden.
         a   garage.
         no

Wie findest du deinen Garten?
Der Garten gefällt mir (wirklich) gut...
                  nicht (besonders gut)...

What do you think of your garden?
I (really)   like the garden...
 don't (particularly)

Wie viele Zimmer gibt es bei euch?
Bei uns gibt es... Zimmer.

Welche Zimmer gibt es?
Unten haben wir... die Küche,
　　　　　　　　das Esszimmer,
　　　　　　　　das Wohnzimmer.
Oben haben wir... zwei / drei Schlafzimmer,
　　　　　　　　das Badezimmer,
　　　　　　　　die Toilette.

Wo ist dein Zimmer?
Mein Zimmer ist im zweiten Stock.
　　　　　　　im ersten Stock.
　　　　　　　im Erdgeschoss.

Mein Zimmer ist neben dem　　Badezimmer.
　　　　　　　gegenüber vom

Wie groß ist dein Zimmer?
Mein Zimmer ist ziemlich groß.
　　　　　　　sehr　　klein.

Welche Farbe hat dein Zimmer?
Die Tapete ist blau und der Teppich ist blau und rosa.

Was gibt es in deinem Zimmer?
In meinem Zimmer gibt es einen Fernseher.
　　　　　　　　　　　　　　roten Teppich.
　　　　　　　　　　　　　　Computer.
　　　　　　　　　　　　　　Stuhl.
　　　　　　　　　　　　　　Schreibtisch.
　　　　　　　　　　　　　　Nachttisch.
　　　　　　　　　　　　　　großen
　　　　　　　　　　　　　　　Kleiderschrank.
　　　　　　　　　　　　eine blaue Kommode.
　　　　　　　　　　　　　　Lampe.
　　　　　　　　　　　　ein　Radio.
　　　　　　　　　　　　　　schwarzes
　　　　　　　　　　　　　　　Bücherregal.
　　　　　　　　　　　　viele Bücher.
　　　　　　　　　　　　　　Posters.

(→*For notes on putting in colours / adjectives see page 130.*)

Auf dem Schreibtisch gibt es　einen Computer.
　　der Kommode　habe ich eine Lampe.
　　dem Bücherregal　　　　ein Radio.
An　der Wand　　　　　　　viele Posters.

How many rooms are there in your house?
In my house there are... rooms.

What rooms are there?
Downstairs we have... the kitchen,
　　　　　　　　　　the dining room,
　　　　　　　　　　the living room.
Upstairs we have... two / three bedrooms,
　　　　　　　　　the bathroom,
　　　　　　　　　the toilet.

Where is your room?
My room is on the second floor.
　　　　　on the first floor.
　　　　　on the ground floor.

My room is next to　the bathroom.
　　　　　opposite

How big is your room?
My room is quite big.
　　　　　very　small.

What colour is your room?
The carpet is blue and the wallpaper is blue and pink.

What is there in your room?
In my room there is a　　　TV.
　　　　　　　　　　　　red carpet.
　　　　　　　　　　　　computer.
　　　　　　　　　　　　chair.
　　　　　　　　　　　　desk.
　　　　　　　　　　　　bedside table.
　　　　　　　　　　　　big wardrobe.

　　　　　　　　　　　　blue chest of drawers.
　　　　　　　　　　　　lamp.
　　　　　　　　　　　　radio.
　　　　　　　　　　　　black bookshelf.

　　　　　　　　　lots of books.
　　　　　　　　　　　　posters.

On the desk　　　　　there is / are a computer.
　the chest of drawers I have　　a lamp.
　the bookshelf　　　　　　　　a radio.
　the wall　　　　　　　　　　lots of posters.

German Revision Guide

Was gibt es im Badezimmer?
Es gibt eine Badewanne, eine Dusche, ein Waschbecken und eine Toilette.

Was gibt es in der Küche?
Es gibt einen Herd, einen Geschirrspülautomat, eine Waschmaschine, ein Spülbecken und einen Kühlschrank.

Was gibt es im Wohnzimmer?
Es gibt einen Fernseher, einen Videorecorder, einen Sessel, ein Sofa, eine Lampe, einen Tisch und vier Stühle.

Wie findest du dein Haus?
Ich finde mein Haus toll.
               okay.
               schrecklich.

What is there in the bedroom?
There's a bath, a shower, a basin and a toilet.

What is there in the kitchen?
There's an oven, a dishwasher, a washing machine, a sink and a fridge.

What is there in the living room?
There's a TV, a video recorder, an armchair, a sofa, a lamp, a table and four chairs.

What do you think of your house?
I think my house is great.
               OK.
               terrible.

Gefällt dir dein Garten?
Ja, er gefällt mir gut,
Nein, er gefällt mir nicht,

weil man dort Fußball spielen kann.
     man sich dort entspannen kann.
     es dort viele Blumen und Bäume gibt.
     er sehr groß / klein ist.

Hast du dein eigenes Schlafzimmer?
Ich habe mein eigenes Schlafzimmer.
Ich teile mein Zimmer mit meinem Bruder.
                        meiner Schwester.
Leider muss ich mein Zimmer mit... teilen!

Mein Zimmer ist klein aber gemütlich.

Wie findest du dein Haus?
Es gefällt mir (nicht),
weil es sehr bequem   ist.
        modern
            zu klein / groß

Do you like the garden?
Yes, I like it,
No, I don't like it,

because you can play football there.
     you can relax there.
     there are lots of flowers and trees there.
     it's very big / small.

Have you got your own bedroom?
I have my own bedroom.
I share my room with my brother.
                        my sister.
Unfortunately I have to share my room with...!

My room is small but cosy.

What do you think of your house?
I (don't) like it,
because it's very comfortable.
          modern.
          too small / big.

Make sure you memorise how to speak and write about your house before you go on to the next section!

(Remember, if you're doing   , you need to understand the boxed bits but you don't need to use them yourself. But if you're doing you need to use the boxed bits.)

28

Slave labour

Downstairs in the kitchen, Gerhard is helping his mother with the evening meal. He is anxious to get into Frau Grün's good books as his girlfriend, Gabi, is coming to stay for the weekend and he would like some money to take her out to the cinema. (He has just blown almost a year's pocket money on a new violin, and is completely broke.)

Read Gerhard's conversation with his mother and use it to help you talk about what chores you and your family do and how much pocket money you get.

Gerhard	Mutti...
Frau Grün	Ja, Gerhard?
Gerhard	Ich helfe viel zu Hause, oder?
Frau Grün	Ich weiß nicht. Was machst du denn?
Gerhard	Also, jeden Tag mache ich mein Bett. Jeden Montag, Mittwoch und Freitag spüle ich ab. Jeden Dienstag und Donnerstag trockne ich ab. Ich räume auch immer mein Zimmer auf...
Frau Grün	Das finde ich normal!
Gerhard	Aber heute habe ich staubgesaugt, und letztes Wochenende habe ich die Fahrräder gewaschen und im Garten geholfen...
Frau Grün	Na und?
Gerhard	Ich möchte heute abend mit Gabi ins Kino gehen.
Frau Grün	Gute Idee!
Gerhard	Aber Mutti, ich habe kein Geld!
Frau Grün	Du bekommst 15 Mark Taschengeld pro Woche.

Gerhard	Das ist nicht genug! Ich muss Kleidung, Musik und alles davon kaufen! Und ich mache mehr als Gretchen. Sie ist wirklich faul. Sie deckt den Tisch und das ist alles!
Frau Grün	Gretchen ist viel jünger als du!
Gerhard	Bitte, Mutti! Wie kann ich dir jetzt helfen? Was kann ich machen?
Frau Grün	Kannst du bitte diese Töpfe abspülen?
Gerhard	Kriege ich dann noch 15 Mark?

Wortautomat

Wie hilfst du zu Hause?	**How do you help around the house?**
Ich decke den Tisch.	I set the table.
Ich staubsauge.	I do the vacuum cleaning.
Ich putze.	I do the cleaning.
Ich wasche die Wäsche.	I wash the clothes.
das Auto.	the car.
den Hund.	the dog.
Ich helfe im Garten.	I help in the garden.
Ich bereite das Mittagessen vor.	I get the lunch ready.
Ich räume den Tisch ab.	I clear the table.
Ich spüle / wasche ab.	I wash up.
Ich trockne ab.	I dry up.
Ich räume mein Zimmer auf.	I tidy my room.
Ich gehe mit dem Hund spazieren.	I walk the dog.

German Revision Guide

To say how often you do things, you have to change the word order:

Jeden Tag	**decke ich** den Tisch.	Every day I set the table
Normalerweise	**putze ich** das Wohnzimmer.	Usually I clean the living room.
Manchmal	**helfe ich** im Garten.	Sometimes I help in the garden.
Ab und zu	**wasche ich** das Auto.	Now and then I wash the car.

(➜ *See page 143 for notes on word order.*)

Was musst du machen? — **What do you have to do?**

Ich muss die Wäsche waschen. — I have to wash the clothes.
        den Tisch decken. — set the table.
        mit dem Hund spazieren gehen. — walk the dog.

(➜ *See page 136 for notes on saying what you must do.*)

Wie viel Taschengeld bekommst du? — **How much pocket money do you get?**

Ich bekomme 5 Pfund Taschengeld pro Woche. — I get £5 pocket money per week.
                    Monat. — month.

Was kaufst du davon? — **What do you buy with it?**

Ich kaufe Kleidung. — I buy clothes.
       Schokolade. — chocolate.
       Süßigkeiten. — sweets.
       Zeitschriften. — magazines.
       Kassetten / CDs. — cassettes / CDs.
Ich gehe ins Kino. — I go to the cinema.
       zum Sportzentrum. — to the sport centre.

When you talk about what other people do, remember to make the verb ending agree with the person/people doing the action: **-t** *or* **-et** *for singular,* **-en** *for plural.*

Was machen die anderen? — **What do the others do?**

(*singular*)
    Mein Vater bereit**et** das Essen vor. — My dad gets the meal ready.
    Meine Mutter deck**t** den Tisch. — My mum sets the table.
    Meine Schwester mach**t** nichts. — My sister does nothing.

(*plural*)
    Meine Brüder spül**en** ab. — My brothers wash up.
    Meine Schwestern helf**en** im Garten. — My sisters help in the garden.

Bekommst du genug Taschengeld? — **Do you get enough pocket money?**

Meine Eltern geben mir genug Taschengeld. — My parents give me enough pocket money.
                nicht genug — don't give me

Ich bekomme ziemlich viel Taschengeld, aber ich muss meine eigene Kleidung kaufen. — I get quite a lot of pocket money, but I have to buy my own clothes.
20 Pfund pro Woche finde ich ziemlich großzügig. — I think £20 a week is quite generous.
5 Pfund ist mir nicht genug, wenn ich meine eigene Kleidung kaufen muss. — £5 isn't enough for me if I have to buy my own clothes.
Das finde ich unfair! — I think that's unfair!

Bei uns

| Wie kann ich (dir) helfen? | How can I help (you)? |
| (Ihnen*) | |

*Say **dir** to a friend, child or member of your family, and say **Ihnen** to an adult.*

Kannst du mir bitte helfen?	Can you help me please?
Kannst du bitte abspülen?	Can you wash up, please?
das Essen vorbereiten?	get the meal ready,
den Tisch decken?	set the table,

Kriege ich dann noch 15 Mark? Do I get another 15 Marks then?

*You might have noticed that one verb can be used to say a lot of different things. It all depends on who does or did it, when, and whether it's something you have to do or a request for help. Take for example **den Tisch decken** (to set the table). You can say...*

Ich decke den Tisch.	I set the table. (*Present*)
Jeden Tag decke ich den Tisch.	Every day I set the table.
Meine Schwester deckt den Tisch.	My sister sets the table.
Meine Eltern decken den Tisch.	My parents set the table.
Ich habe den Tisch gedeckt.	I set the table. (*Past*)
Gestern habe ich den Tisch gedeckt.	Yesterday I set the table.
Ich muss den Tisch decken.	I have to set the table.
Heute muss ich den Tisch decken.	Today I have to set the table.
Kannst du bitte den Tisch decken?	Can you set the table, please?

*If you want to get really good at using different sorts of sentence, the only thing to do is to practise! Write down the first two words of each of the **den Tisch decken** sentences and see how well you can remember the rest of the words. Think about the meaning as you practise. When you're confident, try writing similar sentences using other expressions such as:*

den Tisch abräumen, staubsaugen, putzen,
die Wäsche waschen,
im Garten helfen,
das Essen vorbereiten, abspülen, abtrocknen,
mein Zimmer aufräumen,
mit dem Hund spazieren gehen.

Once you have memorised how to speak and write about jobs round the house and pocket money, get a friend to ask you the questions from the **Wortautomat** and then give you marks out of 10 for how well you answer.

To get a good mark you should:

1 answer the question asked as fully as possible – not just **ja** or **nein**!

2 pronounce the German as accurately as you can.

3 make few or no grammatical mistakes.

4 answer confidently with little hesitation.

5 show initiative – give some extra details that were not specifically asked for.

Another way of doing this would be to write down the questions, then record yourself answering them and mark yourself. If you're not satisfied with your performance, do some more practice and then have another go.

German Revision Guide

Test yourself

Task 1

Conversation: How long can you talk about your house? Use the Mind Map below as a prompt.

Task 2

 Du bekommst einen kurzen Brief aus Deutschland.

Lieber John!

Grüß dich, wie geht's? Mir geht's nicht so gut. Ich habe heute den ganzen Tag zu Hause geholfen, weil mein Vater krank ist. Er hat Grippe und muss drei Tage im Bett bleiben. Am Morgen bin ich einkaufen gegangen, dann habe ich staubgesaugt und das Wohnzimmer aufgeräumt. Ich musste dann das Mittagessen vorbereiten, abwaschen und abtrocknen. Am Nachmittag wollte ich ein paar Stunden Computerspiele machen, aber ich musste mit dem Hund spazierengehen. Danach war ich total kaputt und bin vor dem Fernseher eingeschlafen. Hoffentlich geht's Vati bald besser!

Schreib bald, und sag mir, wie du zu Hause helfen musst!

Dein Rolf.

Richtig, Falsch, oder Nicht im Text?	Richtig	Falsch	Nicht im Text
a) Rolf ist krank.	☐	☐	☐
b) Er hat heute viele Hausaufgaben gemacht.	☐	☐	☐
c) Rolfs Vater liegt im Bett seit drei Tagen.	☐	☐	☐
d) Rolf macht gern Computerspiele.	☐	☐	☐
e) Er hilft normalerweise nicht zu Hause.	☐	☐	☐

You've deserved a breather again. How did you do in Bei uns?

Answers

Task 2: a) Falsch b) Falsch c) Falsch d) Richtig e) Nicht im Text.

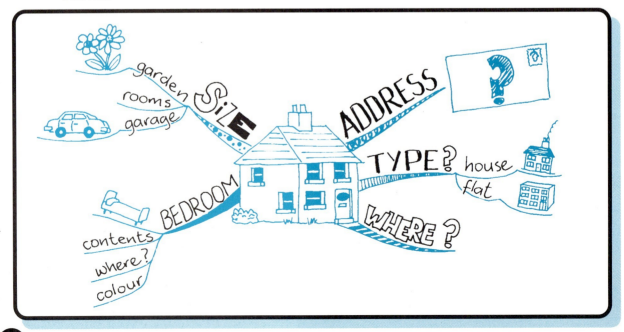

3

Zu Besuch

Gabi checks in

Now it's time to go back to the Grüns' house, where Gabi, Gerhard's incredibly beautiful and talented new girlfriend, has just arrived.

Gerhard	Grüß dich, Gabi, komm herein! Hier ist meine Mutter.
Frau Grün	Guten Tag, Gabi. Wie geht's dir?
Gabi	Ziemlich gut, danke, Frau Grün.
Frau Grün	Setz dich, Gabi. Möchtest du eine Tasse Kaffee?

Zehn Minuten später...

Gabi	So, Gerhard, wo ist mein Zimmer?
Gerhard	Du teilst mit Gretchen – hier, neben dem Badezimmer.
Gabi	Ach so. Darf ich jetzt duschen?
Gerhard	Ja, natürlich. Hast du alles, was du brauchst?
Gabi	Nein. Ich habe kein Handtuch, und ich habe meine Seife vergessen.
Gerhard	Das macht nichts! Du findest alles im Badezimmer!
Gabi	Und wann essen wir heute abend?
Gerhard	Gegen halb sieben.

Gabi	Das ist aber früh! Bei uns essen wir normalerweise um acht Uhr! Und was essen wir genau?
Gerhard	Linseneintopf mit Vollkornbrot.
Gabi	Bei mir essen wir immer Fleisch. Ich finde, das ist wichtig für die Gesundheit.
Gerhard	Wir sind alle Vegetarier.

checklist

What would you say if you had to ...

	Kein Problem!	Hilfe!
FOUNDATION LEVEL		
greet, welcome and introduce a visitor?	○	○
ask if you may have a bath or a shower?	○	○
say you need, and ask someone if they need, soap, toothpaste, towel?	○	○
ask where rooms are in a house?	○	○
say, and ask others, when you have meals?	○	○
ask to use the telephone or radio, or watch television?	○	○
understand simple information and give opinions about newspapers, magazines, TV programmes, radio, music, performers?	○	○
say which programmes or films you have recently seen, or what music you have heard – when and where?	○	○
HIGHER LEVEL		
talk about typical meals, meal-times and eating habits?	○	○
understand and talk about the plot of a book?	○	○
understand and talk about simple news items?	○	○
ask for and give opinions about newspapers, magazines, books, TV programmes, radio, music, performers?	○	○

German Revision Guide

Gabi's manners aren't all they could be, but you will still find her conversation with Gerhard useful. Imagine that you are visiting a German family, and write down how you would greet people and then ask for and talk about similar things.

Wortautomat

Guten Morgen!	Good Morning!
Tag!	Afternoon!
Abend!	Evening
Gute Nacht!	Good night!
Grüss dich!	Hello!
Grüss Gott!	Hello!
Hallo!	Hello!
Servus!	Hello / See you!
Auf Wiedersehen!	Goodbye!
Bis später!	See you later!
Tschüs!	Bye!
Wie geht's?	**How are you?**
Sehr gut, danke.	Very well, thanks.
Ziemlich	Quite
Nicht so	Not so
Und dir?	**And you?**
Ihnen?	
Hier ist meine Mutter.	This is my mum.
Darf ich meinen Bruder vorstellen?	**Can I introduce my brother?**
Komm herein!	Come in!
Kommen Sie herein!	
Setz dich!	Sit down!
Setzen Sie sich!	

Willkommen in Deutschland!	Welcome to Germany!
Vielen Dank für Ihre Gastfreundschaft.	Thanks very much for having me.
Darf ich (jetzt) duschen / baden?	**Can I have a shower / bath (now)?**
Hast du alles, was du brauchst?	**Have you got everything you need?**
Brauchst du etwas?	**Do you need anything?**
Ich habe	I haven't got
keinen Fön.	a hairdryer.
keine Seife.	any soap.
kein Handtuch.	a towel.
Ich habe	I've forgotten
meinen Wecker	my alarm clock.
meine Zahnpasta	my toothpaste.
meine Zahnbürste	my toothbrush.
vergessen.	
Wo ist das Badezimmer, bitte?	**Where's the bathroom, please?**
Wo schlafe ich?	**Where am I going to sleep?**
Wann essen wir?	**When are we eating?**
Um wie viel Uhr ist das Abendessen?	**What time is the evening meal?**
Das Abendessen ist um…	The evening meal is at…
Das Frühstück	Breakfast
Das Mittagessen	Lunch

HIGHER LEVEL

Um wie viel Uhr isst du normalerweise? — **What time do you normally eat?**
Bei uns essen wir normalerweise um sechs Uhr. — In our house we normally eat at six o'clock.
Bei mir… — In my…
(→ See page 100 for telling the time.)

In England essen wir früher als in Deutschland. — In England we eat earlier than in Germany.

Zu Besuch

Was isst du normalerweise zum Frühstück?			**What do you normally have for breakfast?**	
Ich esse Getreideflocken mit Milch und Zucker.			I eat cereal with milk and sugar.	
Toast mit Butter und Orangenmarmelade.			toast with butter and marmalade.	
Ich trinke Tee (mit Milch und Zucker).			I drink tea with (milk and sugar).	
Kaffee.			coffee.	
Orangensaft.			orange juice.	

Was esst ihr zu Abend? — **What do you have for your evening meal?**
Linseneintopf mit Vollkornbrot — Lentil stew with wholemeal bread.

Wir essen	viel	Fisch.	We eat a lot of	fish.
Ich esse	wenig	Käse.	I don't eat much	cheese.
	keinen		don't eat any	

Wir essen	viel	Fleisch.	We eat a lot of	meat.
Ich esse	wenig	Hähnchen.	I don't eat much	chicken.
	kein	Brot.	don't eat any	bread.
		Obst.		fruit.
		Gemüse.		vegetables.

Wir essen	viele	Süßigkeiten.	We eat a lot of	
Ich esse	wenige		I don't eat many	sweets.
	keine		don't eat any	

Ich finde, das ist wichtig für die Gesundheit. — I think it's important for your health.
Joghurt schmeckt mir (nicht). — I (don't) like the taste of yoghurt.
Erbsen schmecken mir (nicht). — I (don't) like the taste of peas..
Ich finde es lecker / ekelhaft / zu salzig / süß. — I find it delicious / disgusting / too salty / sweet.
Ich bin allergisch gegen Käse. — I'm allergic to cheese.
Ich bin Vegetarier(in), also esse ich kein Fleisch. — I'm a vegetarian, so I don't eat any meat.
Ich esse nicht gern Karotten. — I don't like carrots.
(➔ See pages 110–11 for more types of food.)

Don't forget to memorise the phrases you have noted down. A variation on the symbols technique is to cut up some paper into small cards, then write the phrase on one side, and either a symbol or a key word on the other. Turn the cards symbols up, put them in a pile, shuffle, and see if you can remember what is written on the other side. As you go through the cards, sort them into ones you got right and ones you got wrong. Keep testing yourself until they are all in the 'right' pile.

Couch potatoes

Gerhard's mother has firmly refused to give him any more pocket money. Gabi has spent all her spare cash on a new outfit, so the two of them will now have to spend the evening in front of the television. Neither is particularly happy about this, especially as Marlene Müller is planning to have one of her extremely loud parties tonight, and has certainly not invited *them* along…

Gerhard Was für Musik hörst du gern, Gabi?
Gabi Meine Lieblingsgruppe ist Oasis, aber ich höre auch gern Spice Girls.
Gerhard Es tut mir Leid, aber ich habe nur klassische Musik. Möchtest du meine neue Mozart CD hören?

German Revision Guide

Gabi	Nein, danke. Das finde ich sehr langweilig. Was gibt es heute abend im Fernsehen?
Gerhard	Um 20:00 Uhr gibt es die Nachrichten, und dann um 20:15 Uhr gibt es *Star Trek* und um 21:15 Uhr einen Krimi. Was meinst du?
Gabi	Die Nachrichten finde ich sehr interessant, aber *Star Trek* ist doof, und Krimis gefallen mir gar nicht.
Gerhard	Ich habe den Film letztes Jahr im Kino gesehen. Er ist sehr spannend.
Gabi	Darf ich jetzt die Nachrichten sehen?

Gerhard	Ja, aber wir müssen unbedingt diesen Film sehen. Ein Mann lernt eine schöne Frau kennen. Sie verlieben sich, aber dann verschwindet die Frau...

Imagine that you are having a similar conversation with a friend. Write down what you say using the **Wortautomat** to help you.

Wortautomat

Was gibt es heute abend im Fernsehen?
Es gibt einen Film.
Um 19:00 Uhr gibt es einen Krimi.
einen Zeichentrickfilm.
eine Musiksendung.
eine Quizsendung.
eine Komödie.
eine Spielshow.
eine Seifenoper.
die Nachrichten.
den Wetterbericht.

Darf ich (jetzt) meinen Vater anrufen?
meine Mutter
fernsehen?
Radio hören?
Ja, kein Problem!

Welche Sendungen hast du in letzter Zeit gesehen?
Filme
Ich habe *X Files* gesehen.

Was für Musik hast du in letzter Zeit gehört?
Ich habe... gehört.

Was hast du in letzter Zeit gelesen?
Ich habe eine Horrorgeschichte gelesen.

Wo?
Im Kino.
Zu Hause, im Fernsehen.
Ich habe... im Kino gesehen.
Ich bin zu einem Konzert in Manchester gegangen.

What's on TV tonight?
There's a film.
At 7 o'clock there's a thriller.
a cartoon.
a music programme.
a quiz show.
a comedy.
a game show.
a soap opera.
the news.
the weather forecast.

May I ring my Dad (now)?
my Mum
watch TV?
listen to the radio?
Yes, no problem!

Which programmes have you seen recently?
films
I've seen the *X Files*.

What sort of music have you listened to recently?
I've listened to...

What have you read recently?
I've read a horror story.

Where?
At the cinema.
At home, on the TV.
I saw... at the cinema.
I went to a concert in Manchester.

Zu Besuch

Wann?	**When?**
Am Samstag.	On Saturday.
Letztes Wochenende.	Last weekend.
Am Samstag habe ich ... im Kino gesehen.	On Saturday I saw ... at the cinema.
Wie findest du Krimis?	**What do you think of thrillers?**
Horrorfilme?	horror films?
Quizsendungen?	quiz programmes?
Seifenopern?	soap operas?
Krimis finde ich toll.	I think thrillers are great.
Horrorfilme schrecklich.	horror films terrible.
Wie war der Film?	**How was the film?**
die Sendung?	the programme?
Toll!	Great!
Was meinst du?	**What do you think?**
Was für Filme / Sendungen siehst du gern?	**What sort of films / TV programmes do you like watching?**
Ich sehe gern...	I like watching...
Was für Musik hörst du gern?	**What sort of music do you like listening to?**
Ich höre gern...	I like listening to...
Was liest du gern?	**What do you like reading?**
Ich lese gern...	I like reading...
Am liebsten sehe ich...	Best of all I like watching...
höre ich...	I like listening to...
lese ich...	I like reading...
Was ist deine Lieblingsgruppe?	**What's your favourite group?**
Lieblingssendung?	favourite TV programme?
Wer ist dein Lieblingssänger?	**Who's your favourite (male) singer?**
deine Lieblingssängerin?	(female)
Meine Lieblingsgruppe ist...	My favourite group is...
Mein Lieblingssänger	My favourite singer
Meine Lieblingssängerin	

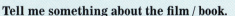

Nach dem Film gibt es einen/eine/ein...	After the film there's a...
Nach der Seifenoper	After the soap
Nach den Nachrichten	After the news
Sag mir etwas über den Film / den Roman.	**Tell me something about the film / book.**
Es geht um eine Frau und einen Mann.	It's about a man and a woman.
Sie lernen sich in einer Bar kennen.	They meet in a bar.
Sie verlieben sich.	They fall in love.
Sie hat ein Verhältnis.	She has an affair.
Er ist eifersüchtig.	He's jealous.
Es gibt einen Unfall.	There's an accident.
Er wird verletzt.	He gets injured.

German Revision Guide

Sie verschwindet.	She disappears.
Er stirbt.	He dies.
bringt ihn/sie um.	kills him/her.
Es ist sehr traurig.	He is very sad.

Ask your teacher for more phrases to talk about your favourite book or film, but remember to keep them simple!

Krimis finde ich toll,	I think thrillers are great
Horrorfilme schrecklich,	horror films terrible
weil sie spannend sind.	because they're exciting.
interessant	interesting.
gruselig	scary.
langweilig	boring.

When you have memorised this section, see how many similar conversations you can improvise. Pretend to be different sorts of people with a variety of tastes in music, reading, films and television. This technique works best if you do it using a different voice for each character. Work with a friend, or a cassette-recorder, or just on your own. Don't worry if you feel silly – this is normal!

Practice

Meanwhile, back at the Grüns', Gerhard and Gabi are not having the best of evenings. Unfortunately, Marlene's party has already started and even with the television at full volume it is almost impossible to hear the newscaster.

Gabi is annoyed that she has missed some of the details and would be very grateful if you could help her out by listening to the news on your cassette and answering her questions.

1 Wie viele Personen sind ins Krankenhaus gefahren worden?

2 Um wie viel Uhr ist der Unfall passiert?

3 Wo war das?

4 Wie viele Personen sind schwer verletzt?

5 Seit wann funktioniert die Verkehrsampel nicht?

6 Wie viele Personen sind gestorben?

Test yourself

Task 1

Katja und Sabine besprechen ihre Lieblingssendungen. Hör zu. Wer sagt das, Katja oder Sabine?

a) „Am Strand" ist nicht sehr interessant.
b) „Am Strand" ist realistisch.
c) „Musik Now" ist eine tolle Sendung.

Richtig oder falsch?   Richtig   Falsch

d) Der Koch in „Am Strand" ist nie gut gelaunt. ☐ ☐
e) Katja findet Musiksendungen interessanter als Seifenopern. ☐ ☐
f) Sabine hat „Musik Now" gestern gesehen. ☐ ☐

Answers

Practice
1 5 – 3 Männer und 2 Frauen; **2** 5.30 Uhr; **3** Verkehrsampel, Siegfriedstraße; **4** 1 Person; **5** Seit 3 Tagen; **6** Keine/Niemand.

Zu Besuch

Task 2

Role-play: your Swiss pen-friend has just arrived. Make her feel at home by welcoming her in German:

a) Greet her.
b) Ask her to come in.
c) Ask how she is.
d) Introduce your mother.
e) Ask her to sit down.

Task 3

Du bist bei einem deutschen Freund und möchtest dich waschen. Was sagst du?

Task 4

Conversation: How long can you talk about your favourite television programmes, films, magazines, music, and performers? Use the Mind Map overleaf as a prompt.

Give reasons for your opinions.

Task 5

Read this advert for a new magazine for teenagers:

Los!
Unsere neue Zeitschrift ist voller Ideen für unternehmungslustige Teenager!
Sport - Musik - Kino - Liebe - Freunde - Gesundheit - Mode
Versuch mal **Los!**

What interest areas does this magazine concentrate on?

Task 6

Lies diese Zusammenfassung von einem neuen Buch für Jugendliche und dann füll die Lücken aus:

„*Sechzehn*" ist ein neues Buch für Teenager, die sich ab und zu nicht so gut mit ihren Eltern verstehen... Beate ist 15 Jahre alt und wohnt mit ihren Eltern in einer Kleinstadt. Beate fühlt sich frustriert, weil sie nie machen darf, was sie will. Abends darf sie nicht ausgehen, denn es sei zu gefährlich für junge Mädchen. Freunde kommen nie zu ihr, denn ihre Eltern sind zu streng. Doch an ihrem sechzehnten Geburtstag lernt Beate einen neuen Freund kennen, und ihr Leben verändert sich für immer...

a) Das Buch heißt ....
b) Es ist für Jugendliche, die manchmal Probleme mit .... haben.
c) Die Hauptperson wohnt in einer kleinen .....
d) Sie .... ausgehen, aber sie .... nicht.
e) Mit .... Jahren findet Beate einen neuen .....

Answers

Task 1
a) Katja; b) Sabine; c) Katja; d) Richtig; e) Richtig; f) Falsch.

Task 2
Model answer: a) Grüß dich! b) Komm herein! c) Wie geht's? d) Hier ist meine Mutter. e) Setz dich!

Task 3
a) Darf ich duschen? b) Wo ist das Badezimmer? c) Ich habe keine Seife und kein Handtuch.

Task 5
sport, music, cinema, love, friends, health, fashion.

Task 6
a) *Sechzehn*; b) ihren Eltern; c) Stadt; d) will / möchte, darf; e) 16, Freund.

German Revision Guide

Task 7

A survey: What do your friends like watching on TV? Add four more types of programme to the list.

Musiksendungen

Krimis

....

....

....

....

Task 8

Was isst man bei dir? Schreib einen Artikel für ein deutsches Schulmagazin. In deinem Artikel musst du folgendes erwähnen:

– was du gern / nicht gern isst – und warum;

– um wie viel Uhr und was du normalerweise isst (zum Frühstück / zu Mittag / zu Abend);

– ob du deutsches Essen schon probiert hast;

– wenn ja, wie du das gefunden hast.

Task 8 — Model answer

Ich esse gern Fleisch, Pommes frites und Schokolade, weil sie gut schmecken, aber sie sind nicht sehr gesund, also esse ich sie nicht sehr oft. Salat und Gemüse finde ich langweilig, aber wichtig für die Gesundheit, also esse ich sie jeden Tag. Schrecklich!

Normalerweise frühstücke ich um Viertel vor acht: Cornflakes mit Milch und Zucker und eine Tasse Tee oder manchmal Kaffee. Ich esse gegen ein Uhr zu Mittag. Meistens esse ich ein Käsebrot mit Tomaten und dann einen Joghurt. Das Abendessen ist um sechs Uhr. Wir essen viel Fisch mit Kartoffeln und Gemüse – Karotten oder Erbsen.

Ich habe letztes Jahr deutsches Essen probiert. Ich bin im Juli mit der Schule nach Koblenz gefahren. Das Essen im Hotel war ziemlich gut, aber ich finde, man isst zuviel Schweinefleisch und es gibt wenig für Vegetarier. Wir haben auch Kaffee und Kuchen in einem Café probiert. Das war wirklich lecker!

4 Schule stinkt!

Day in the life ...

It's seven o'clock on Monday morning and Martin Müller is filled with dread at the thought of having to get out of bed and face another week at school. One of his problems is that he doesn't have a very good sense of time. Read what he does on a typical school day and then help him to get organised by filling in what time he does everything from the list below. Clue: he's usually late for school. (The first time has been filled in to get you started.)

Der Wecker klingelt um __e)__ Ich schlafe wieder ein, und wache um ___ auf.

Ich stehe auf, frühstücke in der Küche, wasche mich, putze mir die Zähne und ziehe meine Jeans und ein T-Shirt an.

Dann suche ich meine Schulmappe. Oft kann ich sie nicht finden.

Um ___ gehe ich zur Bushaltestelle. Der Bus kommt um ___, und ich komme normalerweise gegen ___ in der Schule an.

Die Schule beginnt um ___ und ist um ___ aus – schrecklich! Wir haben fünf Stunden pro Tag, und nur eine Pause, von ___ bis ___.

Nach der Schule essen wir zu Mittag, und dann mache ich meine Hausaufgaben bis ___ – so langweilig!

Nach dem Abendessen sehe ich fern.

Um ___ gehe ich ins Bett und mache Computerspiele.

a) fünf nach acht
b) zwanzig vor acht
c) halb zwölf
d) elf Uhr
e) Viertel vor sieben
f) Mitternacht
g) sechs Uhr
h) sieben Uhr
i) halb zwei
j) acht Uhr
k) Viertel vor acht

checklist

What would you say if you had to ...

Foundation

	Kein Problem!	Hilfe!
talk about a typical school day?	○	○
talk about homework?	○	○
ask for help in the classroom?	○	○
say you don't know?	○	○
ask whether, or say that, something is wrong?	○	○
ask and talk about school subjects and facilities?	○	○
say what you think of school, and why?	○	○
ask and talk about after-school and lunch-time activities.	○	○

Higher

ask someone to explain a word?	○	○
ask how something is pronounced?	○	○
say how long you have been learning German and any other languages?	○	○
talk about rules and uniform?	○	○
understand about different types of school?	○	○

German Revision Guide

4

Answers j) (g) (h) (q) (k) (a) (j) (l) (d) (c) (f) (e)

Now it's your turn to write down what you have to do on a typical school day. Use what Martin says and the **Wortautomat** to help you. If you can't remember how to say the time in German, look at page 100 before you start.

Wortautomat

Was machst du vor der Schule?
Der Wecker klingelt.
Ich wache um… auf.
Ich stehe auf.
Ich wasche mich.
Ich dusche.
Ich frühstücke.
Ich putze mir die Zähne.

Wie kommst du zur Schule?
Ich gehe um… zur   Schule.
                   Bushaltestelle.
              zum Bahnhof.

Ich gehe zu Fuß   zur Schule.
Ich fahre mit dem Bus
                  Auto
                  Zug
                  Rad
          mit der U-Bahn

Im Winter fahre ich mit dem Bus.
Im Sommer fahre ich mit dem Rad.

Um wie viel Uhr kommst du in der Schule an?
Ich komme um… in der Schule an.

Wann beginnt die Schule?
     ist die Schule aus?
Die Schule beginnt um…
           ist um… aus.

Wie viele Stunden habt ihr am Tag?
Wir haben fünf Stunden am Tag.

Wie lange dauert eine Stunde?
Eine Stunde dauert 50 Minuten.

Wie viele Pausen gibt es?
Es gibt zwei Pausen.

Die erste   Pause ist von… bis…
    zweite

What do you do before school?
The alarm rings.
I wake up at…
I get up.
I have a wash.
I have a shower.
I have breakfast.
I clean my teeth.

How do you get to school?
I go to school   at…
           to the bus stop
           to the station

I go by foot   to school.
        bus
        car
        train
        bike
        underground

In winter I go by bus.
In summer I go by bike.

What time do you get to school?
I get to school at…

When does school begin?
                  end?
School begins at…
       ends

How many lessons do you have a day?
We have five lessons a day.

How long does a lesson last?
A lesson lasts 50 minutes.

How many breaks are there?
There are two breaks.

The first   break is from… to…
    second

Schule stinkt!

Was isst du zu Mittag?
Die Mittagspause dauert eine Stunde.
Normalerweise esse ich ein Käsebrot mit Chips und einen Joghurt.

Was machst du nach der Schule?
Nach der Schule gehe / fahre ich nach Hause.
Ich mache meine Hausaufgaben.
Ich sehe fern.
Ich lese Zeitschriften.
Ich mache Computerspiele.
Ich spiele Fußball.

Vor   dem Abendessen mache ich…
Nach   lese ich…

Ich gehe um… ins Bett.

What do you eat for lunch?
The lunch break lasts for an hour.
Normally I eat a cheese sandwich with crisps and a yoghurt.

What do you do after school?
After school I go home.
I do my homework.
I watch TV.
I read magazines.
I play computer games.
I play football.

Before tea / supper I do…
After   I read…

I go to bed at…

To memorise your daily routine, it might be helpful to note down the times you do things and use them as prompts. Of course, you don't need to actually say what time you do everything.

To make things flow better, use expressions such as **dann** *and* **nach der Schule** *– but remember, they change the word order! E.g.*

7:30   Ich wache um halb acht auf.
7:35   Dann **stehe ich** auf.

English spoken here

It's shortly after 8 o'clock and Marlene Müller, who is just as lazy as her brother, is attempting to sleep her way through an English lesson. Her teacher, however, a dynamic young man called Herr Hock, is having none of it.

Herr Hock	Marlene. Wake up!
Marlene	Wie bitte?
Herr Hock	No sleeping.
Marlene	Ich verstehe nicht. Wie heißt *sleeping* auf Deutsch?
Herr Hock	Marlene, what time did you go to bed last night?
Marlene	Ich weiß es nicht.
Herr Hock	In English, please.
Marlene	Darf ich auf die Toilette gehen?
Herr Hock	Certainly not!

Marlene finally gives in and opens her books. Luckily, she is sitting next to Lotte Marx, who always comes top in everything.

Marlene	Wie heißt *favourite* auf Deutsch? Heißt das **Liebe**?
Lotte	Nein, das ist falsch. Es heißt **Lieblings-**.
Marlene	Wie sagt man **Ich liebe Gerhard Grün**?
Lotte	*I love Gerhard Grün*. Stimmt das?
Marlene	Nein. Wie schreibt man *love*?
Herr Hock	Marlene, wie sagt man *detention* auf Deutsch?

German Revision Guide

Wortautomat

Darf ich	May I
auf die Toilette gehen?	go to the toilet?
das Fenster	open / shut the
aufmachen / zumachen?	window?
Ich verstehe (nicht).	I (don't) understand.
Wie, bitte?	**Pardon?**
Wiederholen Sie*	Repeat that, please.
es, bitte.	
Wiederhole es, bitte.	

Wie schreibt man das?	How do you write that?
Sprechen Sie*	Do you speak
Sprichst du	
Englisch / Deutsch?	English / German?
Wie heißt das auf	What's that in English?
Englisch?	
Was bedeutet das?	What does that mean?
Wie sagt man das	How do you say that
auf Deutsch?	in German?
Ich weiß es nicht.	I don't know.
Stimmt das?	**Is that right / true?**
Das ist richtig / falsch.	That's right / wrong.

Wie buchstabiert man das?	How do you spell that?
Wie spricht man dieses Wort aus?	How do you pronounce this word?
Können Sie* bitte dieses Wort erklären?	Can you explain this word please?
Kannst du diesen Satz	this sentence

*Remember to use **Sie** when you're talking to an adult you don't know, and **du** when you're talking to a friend or a child.

A helpful hint

A good tip for long sentences is to practise them by saying the last word, then the last two words, and so on, adding words until you get back to the beginning, by which time you should know the whole sentence. You might sound something like this:

erklären
Wort erklären
dieses Wort erklären
bitte dieses Wort erklären
Sie bitte dieses Wort erklären
Können Sie bitte dieses Wort erklären?

School rules!

It's 4.30 in the afternoon. Gerhard Grün has finished his homework and is reading a letter from his English pen-friend, Tracy Turner. Tracy's German teacher edits a magazine which publishes articles written in German by her own pupils and their pen-friends. This term she is asking for articles on school life in Germany and Britain. Tracy wants Gerhard to write about his school first so that she can use some of the same expressions in her own article.

After some thought, Gerhard starts to write...

> Hallo! Ich bin Gerhard Grün und ich bin im Jahrgang zehn. Ich besuche eine große gemischte Gesamtschule in Kippenstadt. Wir haben mehr als tausend Schüler und Schülerinnen und ungefähr achtzig Lehrer und Lehrerinnen. Die Schule hat eine gute Atmosphäre, denn die Lehrer sind sehr freundlich und hilfsbereit.
>
> Ich gehe gern in die Schule, denn man kann hier viel Sport treiben. Es gibt einen großen Sportplatz, vier Tennisplätze und eine Turnhalle. Nach der Schule kann man Federball oder Fußball spielen.
>
> Ich lerne Deutsch, Englisch, Mathe, Naturwissenschaften, Informatik, Französisch, Kunst, Geschichte und Erdkunde.

Fremdsprachen gefallen mir wirklich gut und ich bekomme meistens gute Noten in Französisch, aber ich finde Englisch einfacher!

Mein Lieblingsfach ist Musik, und ich bin Mitglied im Schulorchester.

Ich spiele seit sechs Jahren Geige.

Die Schulregeln finde ich gerecht. Wir müssen immer pünktlich und höflich sein und wir dürfen in der Schule nicht rauchen. Wir müssen keine Schuluniform tragen.

In Deutschland endet der Schultag früher als in Großbritannien, aber wir müssen um acht Uhr beginnen! Wer möchte tauschen?

Wortautomat

Was für eine Schule besuchst du?
Ich besuche
  eine (gemischte) Gesamtschule (für Jungen / Mädchen)
  eine Realschule
  eine Privatschule
  ein (gemischtes) Gymnasium

*(In Germany, there is also the **Hauptschule**, which concentrates on vocational or work-orientated qualifications.)*

What sort of school do you go to?
I go to a (mixed) comprehensive (for boys / girls).
  high school
  private school
  grammar school

Wie viele Schüler und Schülerinnen
          Lehrer und Lehrerinnen
 gibt es in deiner Schule?
Es gibt ungefähr 850 Schüler(innen).
Wir haben mehr als 50 Lehrer(innen).

How many pupils
          teachers
 are there in your school?
There are about 850 pupils.
We have more than 50 teachers.

Wie findest du deine Schule?
Ich gehe (nicht) gern in die Schule, denn...
...die Lehrer sind freundlich und hilfsbereit.
...ich habe dort viele / wenige Freunde / Freundinnen.
...ich finde es interessant / langweilig.
...es gibt eine gute Atmosphäre.

What do you think of your school?
I (don't) like going to school because...
...the teachers are friendly and helpful.
...I have lots of / not many friends there.

...I find it interesting / boring.
...there's a good atmosphere.

Was für Sportmöglichkeiten gibt es?
Die Sportmöglichkeiten sind ausgezeichnet.

Man kann dort viel Sport treiben.
Nach der Schule kann man Fußball spielen.
In der Mittagspause

Es gibt einen (großen) Sportplatz.
      eine (große) Turnhalle.
      Tennisplätze.

What sort of sports facilities are there?
The sports facilities are excellent.

You can do lots of sport there.
After school you can play football.
At lunch-time

There is / are a (big) playing field.
      a (big) gym.
      tennis courts.

Was machst du nach der Schule | **What do you do after school?**
      in der Mittagspause? | **at lunch-time?**

Ich spiele Federball in der Turnhalle.
Ich bin Mitglied in der Fußballmannschaft.
    im Schulorchester.

I play badminton in the gym.
I'm a member of the football team.
    school orchestra.

Was ist dein Lieblingsfach?
Welches Fach gefällt dir nicht?
Wie findest du Deutsch?

What's your favourite subject?
Which subject don't you like?
What do you think of German?

Mein Lieblingsfach ist...
Meine Lieblingsfächer sind...
    Deutsch
    Französisch
    Spanisch
    Englisch
    Mathe
    Informatik
    Geschichte
    Erdkunde
    Religion
    Naturwissenschaften
    Biologie
    Chemie
    Physik
    Hauswirtschaft
    Kunst
    Werken
    Sport

My favourite subject is...
My favourite subjects are...
    German
    French
    Spanish
    English
    Maths
    IT
    History
    Geography
    RE
    Science
    Biology
    Chemistry
    Physics
    Home Economics
    Art
    CDT (combined design and technology)
    Sport

Der Lehrer / Die Lehrerin ist sehr nett / unfreundlich.

The teacher is very nice / unfriendly.

Ich finde Deutsch interessant.
        langweilig.
        einfach.
        schwierig.
        interessanter als...
        langweiliger als...
        einfacher als...
        schwieriger als...

I find German interesting.
        boring.
        easy.
        difficult.
        more interesting than...
        more boring than...
        easier than...
        more difficult than...

Ich bekomme (meistens) gute Noten in...
        schlechte

I get (mostly) good marks in...
        bad

Ich mag Werken (nicht).

I (don't) like CDT.

Englisch gefällt mir (überhaupt) nicht.
Fremdsprachen gefallen mir (wirklich) gut.

I (really) don't like English
I (really) like languages.

Schule stinkt!

Wie lange lernst du schon Deutsch?
      spielst   Geige?

Ich lerne Deutsch seit drei Jahren.
Ich spiele Geige seit sechs Jahren.

How long have you been learning German?
      playing the violin?

I've been learning German for three years.
    playing the violin for six years.

Trägst du eine Uniform?
Ja, ich trage einen ...en* Rock.
        eine ...e   Krawatte.
                 Bluse.
                 Hose.
                 Jacke.
        ein ...es   Hemd.
                 Sweatshirt.
        ...e   Socken.
                 Schuhe.

Do you wear a uniform?
Yes, I wear (a)... skirt.
              tie.
              blouse.
              trousers.
              blazer.
              shirt.
              sweatshirt.
              socks.
              shoes.

Nein, ich trage keine Uniform.

No, I don't wear a uniform.

*Put in colour or adjective and remember to add **-en**, **-e**, or **-es**.*
Ich trage ein weiß**es** Hemd und eine gestreif**te** Krawatte.
(➜See page 106 for colours.)

Wie findest du die Schulregeln?
Die Schulregeln finde ich gerecht.
                          ungerecht.

What do you think of the school rules?
I find the school rules fair.
                    unfair.

Wir müssen* eine Uniform tragen.
           pünktlich und höflich sein.
           zwei Stunden Hausaufgaben pro
           Tag machen.

We have to wear a uniform.
          be punctual and polite.
          do two hours of homework per day.

Wir dürfen keinen Kaugummi kauen.
           nicht rauchen.
           nicht im Klassenzimmer essen
           oder trinken.

We're not allowed to chew gum.
          smoke.
          eat or drink in the
          classroom.

*Remember that **Wir müssen nicht / kein** means **We don't have to**.

Wer möchte tauschen?

Who'd like to swap?

Using the symbols technique, memorise what you have written and then test yourself to see how well you've learnt it.

German Revision Guide

Test yourself

Task 1

Conversation: How long can you keep talking about school? Use the Mind Map below to give you some ideas.

 Add rules and uniform to the Mind Map.

Task 2

An advert for a school Open Day:

> Besuchen Sie unsere Realschule für Jungen!
> Am ersten November von 08:00 bis 13:00.
> Kommen Sie in unsere schönen Klassenzimmer und sehen Sie sich echten Unterricht an!
> Sprechen Sie mit Lehrern und Schülern!
> Wir haben:
> ★ Ausgezeichnete Sportmöglichkeiten;
> ★ Eine große Bibliothek;
> ★ Ein Informatikzimmer mit 30 Computern;
> ★ Schöne Gebäude;
> ★ Hilfreiche Lehrer und erfolgreiche Schüler!

Richtig oder falsch?   Richtig Falsch
In dieser Schule...
a) gibt es Mädchen.   ☐ ☐
b) gibt es viele Bücher.   ☐ ☐
c) gibt es eine gute Kantine.   ☐ ☐
d) kann man Sport treiben.   ☐ ☐
e) gibt es keine Computer.   ☐ ☐

Task 3

Ein Brief aus einer Zeitschrift

> Liebe Marion!
> Hilfe! Ich habe ständig Ärger mit meinen Lehrern. Sie mögen mich nicht und geben mir immer schlechte Noten. Sie sagen, daß ich besser aufpassen und weniger herumspielen muss, aber ich finde alle Fächer außer Sport sehr langweilig. Deutsch ist am schlimmsten! Oft verstehe ich meine Hausaufgaben nicht, und dann werden die Lehrer böse! Ich weiß nicht, was ich machen soll. Ich bin so deprimiert!

a) Helga hat viele / wenige Probleme in der Schule.
b) Sie bekommt nie gute / schlechte Noten.
c) Die Lehrer sagen, dass Helga besser zuhören / herumspielen sollte.
d) Helgas Lieblingfach ist Deutsch / Sport.
e) Wenn sie ihre Hausaufgaben nicht versteht, helfen ihr die Lehrer / sind die Lehrer schlecht gelaunt.

Answers

Task 2
a) ✗; b) ✓; c) ✗; d) ✓; e) ✗

Task 3
a) viele; b) gute; c) zuhören; d) Sport; e) sind die Lehrer schlecht gelaunt.

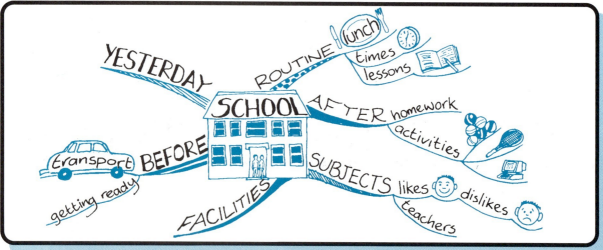

5 An die Arbeit

Just the job

At the **Grundschule**, Martin and Gretchen's teacher has asked the pupils to do a project on different types of jobs. Gretchen has just made up a wordsearch with 18 professions and places of work. When you have found them, use the words to fill in the list below. Some of the jobs are in their masculine form and others are in their feminine form. Make sure you put each word in the right column.

```
I A F A B R I K F H F
N K K A U F F R A U J
G C O R T N R A L V Z
E O C Ä Z I I N E E S
N N H T R T S K H R S
I I Z E A Z E E R K O
E T U R O R U N E Ä L
U S H K B Ä R P R U S
R I A E G N L F P F T
F Z U S C H U L E E I
I I S D L A D E N R E
M L E N A Z P G U I B
G O R Ü B N I E S X R
V P H A U S F R A U A
```

man	/ woman	
_____	/ _____	= businessman / woman
_____	/ _____	= cook
_____	/ _____	= dentist
_____	/ _____	= doctor
_____	/ _____	= engineer
_____	/ _____	= hairdresser
_____	/ _____	= house-husband / housewife
_____	/ _____	= nurse
_____	/ _____	= policeman / woman
_____	/ _____	= salesman / woman
_____	/ _____	= secretary
_____	/ _____	= shop
_____	/ _____	= teacher

_____ = at home   _____ = office
_____ = factory   _____ = school
_____ = unemployed

checklist

What would you say if you had to ...

Foundation Level

	Kein Problem!	Hilfe!
understand and talk about different jobs and work experience?	●	●
understand and talk about your future plans?	●	●
talk about travel to and from work?	●	●
ask for and give a phone number?	●	●
answer and make a phone call?	●	●
take or leave a simple phone message?	●	●

Higher Level

	Kein Problem!	Hilfe!
ask what people do for a living?	●	●
understand and talk about your choice of study or training?	●	●
understand information about different types of further education and training?	●	●
make arrangements to call, and be called, by phone?	●	●
ask to change coins for the phone or buy a phone-card?	●	●

German Revision Guide

Before you check your answers, there's one more thing to do. Because jobs can be done by both men and women, most words for professions have a masculine and a feminine form. To make the feminine, you usually just add **-in** to the masculine form (**Sekretär** / **Sekretärin**). Occasionally you add an umlaut ¨ (**Arzt** / **Ärztin**), or you change **-mann** to **-frau** (**Kaufmann** / **Kauffrau**).

Look through your list and put in both forms of each profession. Then check your answers.

Now read what Martin has to say about his parents' work and his own professional ambitions.

Answers

businessman / woman – **Kaufmann** / **Kauffrau**;
cook – **Koch** / **Köchin**; dentist – **Zahnarzt** / **Zahnärztin**;
doctor – **Arzt** / **Ärztin**, engineer – **Ingenieur(in)**;
hairdresser – **Friseur** / **Friseuse**; househusband / wife – **Hausmann** / **Hausfrau**; nurse – **Krankenpfleger** / **Krankenschwester**; policeman / woman – **Polizist(in)**;
salesman / woman – **Verkäufer(in)**; secretary – **Sekretär(in)**; shop – **Laden**; teacher – **Lehrer(in)**;
at home – **zu Hause**; factory – **Fabrik**; office – **Büro**;
school – **Schule**; unemployed – **arbeitslos**

 Meine Mutter ist Mechanikerin; sie arbeitet bei BMW.

Mein Vater ist Koch. Er arbeitet in einem großen Restaurant in der Stadt.

Meine Schwester ist Schülerin.

 Mutti findet die Arbeit interessant, weil sie sehr praktisch ist. Der Lohn ist ziemlich gut, aber die Arbeit ist anstrengend.

Vati findet die Arbeit schrecklich, denn er arbeitet nicht gern mit anderen Leuten. Er versteht sich nicht gut mit den Kellnern.

Marlene möchte Sängerin werden. Das ist interessant, aber sie kann nicht sehr gut singen.

Wenn ich groß bin, möchte ich Astronaut werden und auf dem Mond wohnen.

Now write about what members of your family do, using Martin's answer, the **Wortautomat** and your wordsearch vocab list to help you.

Wortautomat

Was macht   deine Mutter?
              dein Vater?
      machen deine Eltern?

Meine Mutter ist Mechanikerin*.
Mein Vater ist Koch*.
Meine Eltern sind arbeitslos.

*Don't put **eine** or **ein** in front of the job.

Wo arbeitet er / sie?
Er / Sie arbeitet in einem Büro.
                        Laden.
           in einer   Fabrik.

What does your mum do?
               dad
What do your parents do?

My mum's a mechanic.
My dad's a cook.
My parents are out of work.

Where does he / she work?
He / She works in an office.
                 a shop.
                 a factory.

An die Arbeit

Bank.	a bank.
Schule.	a school.
bei BMW.	at BMW.
zu Hause.	at home.

Wie findet er / sie die Arbeit? **How does he/she find the work?**
Er / Sie findet die Arbeit interessant, He/She finds the work interesting
langweilig, boring
toll, great
schrecklich, terrible

weil er/sie (nicht) sehr praktisch ist. because he / she is(n't) very practical.
gut mit Kindern is good with children.
freundlich is friendly.

Der Lohn ist ziemlich gut / nicht besonders gut. The pay is quite / not particularly good.

Er / Sie arbeitet (nicht) gern mit anderen Leuten. He/She likes/doesn't like working with other people.
Er / Sie versteht sich (nicht) gut gets on well/badly

Was möchtest du werden? **What would you like to be?**
Ich möchte Astronaut werden. I'd like to be an astronaut.

Experience needed

At the **Gesamtschule**, Frau Schmidt is about to start organising work experience placements for pupils in **Jahrgang 10**. To enable them to get the most out of this, she first needs to interview the pupils to discover whether they have any previous experience of working and what their plans for the future are. After interviewing Marlene Müller, who is determined to do her work experience in a large recording studio, Frau Schmidt welcomes Gerhard Grün.

Frau Schmidt	Hallo, Gerhard, wie geht's dir?
Gerhard	Gut, danke.
Frau Schmidt	So, was sind deine Zukunftspläne? Bleibst du hier auf der Schule?
Gerhard	Ja, sicher. Ich werde Musik und Fremdsprachen in der Oberstufe lernen.
Frau Schmidt	Und nach dem Abitur?
Gerhard	Ich weiß noch nicht. Aber ich interessiere mich für Sport und Gesundheit.

Frau Schmidt	Hast du schon einen Job?
Gerhard	Nein, aber letzten Sommer habe ich in einem vegetarischen Restaurant gearbeitet.
Frau Schmidt	Hat es dir gefallen?
Gerhard	Ja, sehr. Ich habe meistens in der Küche geholfen. Es war zu heiß, aber die Arbeit hat Spaß gemacht. Ich habe vier Stunden pro Tag gearbeitet: von 18 bis 22 Uhr.
Frau Schmidt	Und wie viel Geld hast du dabei verdient?
Gerhard	DM10 pro Stunde.
Frau Schmidt	Also gut. Wo möchtest du dein Arbeitspraktikum machen?
Gerhard	Am liebsten in einem Laden oder vielleicht im Sportzentrum.

Imagine that Frau Schmidt is interviewing you about your work experience and plans for the future. Write down the conversation and then memorise it using the symbols or key words technique to help you.

Wortautomat

Was sind deine Zukunftspläne?	**What are your future plans?**
Ich bleibe auf der Schule.	I'm staying at school.
Ich verlasse die Schule.	I'm leaving school.
Ich gehe auf die Hochschule.	I'm going to college.

Ich werde   Musik in der Oberstufe lernen.   I'm going to   study music in the Sixth Form.
Ich möchte   eine Stelle als Kellnerin finden.   I'd like to   find a job as a waitress.

Nach dem Abitur möchte ich auf die Uni gehen.   After my A-levels I'd like to go to university.

Ich möchte Buchhalter(in) werden.   I'd like to become an accountant.

Hast du einen Job?   **Have you got a job?**
Ja, ich arbeite in einem   Supermarkt.   Yes, I work in a supermarket.
                      Laden.   shop.

Ich trage Zeitungen aus.   I deliver newspapers.
Ich mache Babysitting.   I do babysitting.
Ich arbeite als Kellner in einem Restaurant.   I work as a waiter in a restaurant.
Ich habe keinen Job.   I haven't got a job.

Wie kommst du zur Arbeit?   **How do you get to work?**
Ich gehe zu Fuß.   I walk.
Ich fahre mit dem Bus.   I go by bus.
(➜ *See page 42 for more examples.*)

Wie lange dauert die Fahrt?   **How long does the journey take?**
Die Fahrt zur Arbeit dauert ungefähr 20 Minuten.   The journey takes about 20 minutes.

Wie viele Stunden pro Tag arbeitest du?   **How many hours a day do you work?**
Ich arbeite acht Stunden pro Tag: Von 09:00 bis 17:00 Uhr.   I work eight hours a day: from 9 to 5.

Wie viel Geld verdienst du?   **How much money do you earn?**
Ich bekomme 3 Pfund pro Stunde.   I get £3 an hour.

Wie findest du die Arbeit?   **How do you find the work?**
Ich finde die Arbeit interessant.   I find the work interesting.
Die Arbeit ist langweilig, aber ich brauche das Geld.   The work is boring, but I need the money.

Was musst du bei der Arbeit machen?   **What do you have to do at work?**
Ich muss an der Kasse arbeiten.   I have to work on the till.
           den Kunden helfen.   help the customers.
           abspülen.   wash up.
           Anrufe beantworten*.   answer the phone.

You can put all these expressions into the past by saying **Ich musste (I had to) instead of **Ich muss**. If you want to look up another activity in the dictionary, remember to put the infinitive (verb) at the end – in German you say I must at the till **help** or I must in the garden **work**.*

An die Arbeit

Hast du ein Arbeitspraktikum gemacht?	**Have you done a work experience placement?**
Ja, ich habe zwei Wochen in einem Geschäft gearbeitet.	Yes, I worked two weeks in a shop.
Was hast du gemacht?	**What did you do?**
Ich habe an der Kasse gearbeitet.	I worked on the till.
den Kunden geholfen.	I helped customers.
abgespült.	I washed up.
Anrufe beantwortet.	I answered the phone.
Wie hast du die Arbeit gefunden?	**How did you find the work?**
Es hat (keinen) Spaß gemacht.	It was (no) fun.
Es war toll!	It was great!
zu heiß in der Küche.	too hot in the kitchen.
sehr anstrengend.	very tiring.
(➜ See page 141 for more on the perfect tense.)	
Wie viele Stunden hast du jeden Tag gearbeitet?	**How many hours a day did you work?**
Ich habe acht Stunden pro Tag gearbeitet: Von 09:00 bis 17:00 Uhr.	I worked eight hours a day: from 9 to 5.
Warum willst du auf die Uni gehen?	**Why do you want to go to university?**
die Schule verlassen?	**leave school?**
Ich will Arzt(Ärztin) werden.	I want to become a doctor.
Ich möchte Fremdsprachen studieren.	I'd like to study modern languages.
Ich will sofort eine Stelle finden.	I want to find a job straight away.
Warum willst du Rechtsanwalt(-wältin) werden?	**Why do you want to be a lawyer?**
Sänger(in)	**singer?**
Lehrer(in)	**teacher?**
Ich will viel Geld verdienen.	I want to earn lots of money.
Ich arbeite gern mit Kindern.	I like working with children.
Ich möchte anderen Leuten helfen.	I'd like to help other people.
Ich möchte viel Verantwortung haben.	I'd like to have a lot of responsibility.
Ich möchte berühmt werden.	I'd like to be famous.
Hast du andere Zukunftspläne?	**Do you have other plans for the future?**
Ich werde eine Weltreise machen.	I am going to travel the world
Ich möchte heiraten und viele Kinder haben.	I'd like to marry and have lots of children.
Ich möchte im Ausland wohnen.	I'd like to live abroad.

Having discussed his plans with Frau Schmidt, Gerhard is now trying to arrange a placement in either a health food shop or a sports centre. Frau Schmidt has given him a list of useful names and phone numbers, and he's just called the first one.

Frau	Guten Morgen, Karins Bioladen.
Gerhard	Ich möchte bitte Frau Kohl sprechen.
Frau	Sie ist im Moment nicht da.
Gerhard	Können Sie ihr etwas ausrichten?
Frau	Einen Augenblick, bitte... Ja?
Gerhard	Mein Name ist Gerhard Grün, und ich suche ein Arbeitspraktikum für die zweite Woche im Juni. Ich bin Vegetarier und sehr fleißig. Kann sie mich zurück rufen?
Frau	Wie ist ihre Telefonnummer, Herr Grün?
Gerhard	19 45 24
Frau	Wann soll sie zurück rufen?

German Revision Guide

Gerhard	Ich bin bis 11:30 Uhr da.
Frau	Alles klar. Auf Wiederhören.
Gerhard	Vielen Dank. Auf Wiederhören.

Using his phone call to Karins Bioladen and the **Wortautomat** to help you, imagine Gerhard's conversations with two other organisations: *Franks Fitness-Zentrum*, owned by Herr Fischer, and *Das Grüne Blatt*, an organic food shop managed by Frau Honig.

For each dialogue, use as many different expressions as you can.

Wortautomat

Kennen Sie die Vorwahl?
Guten Morgen / Tag / Abend.
Ich möchte bitte mit Herrn Wörner sprechen.
              Frau Kohl
Darf ich mit Herrn Seiser sprechen, bitte?
      Frau Zimmermann
Ist Gabi da?
Am Apparat.
Einen Augenblick, bitte.
Ich versuche, Sie zu verbinden.
Er / Sie ist im Moment nicht da.
Kann er / sie mich zurück rufen?
Wie ist Ihre Telefonnummer?
neunzehn, fünfundvierzig, vierundzwanzig
(*Remember that Germans say phone numbers in pairs of figures.*)
Wann soll er / sie zurück rufen?
Ich bin bis halb zwölf da.
Können Sie ihm / ihr etwas ausrichten?
Sagen Sie ihm / ihr, daß Frau Schäfer angerufen hat.
Auf Wiederhören.

Do you know the dialling code?
Good morning / afternoon / evening.
I'd like to speak to Mr Wörner, please.
              Mrs Kohl
May I speak to Mr Seiser, please?
      Mrs Zimmermann
Is Gabi there?
Speaking.
One moment, please.
I'm trying to connect you.
He / She isn't there at the moment.
Can he / she ring me back?
What's your phone number?
19 45 24

When should he / she ring back?
I'll be here till 11.30.
Can you give him / her a message?
Tell him / her that Mrs Schäfer rang.
Bye (on phone).

Wann kann ich ihn / sie zurück rufen?
Haben Sie Kleingeld für das Telefon?
Ich habe nur einen Zehnmarkschein.
Verkaufen Sie Telefonkarten?

When can I ring him / her back?
Have you got any change for the phone?
I've only got a 10 mark note.
Do you sell phone cards?

Practise reading the dialogues aloud with a friend until you know the expressions without having to look. Then try improvising a couple more; see how long you can keep the conversations going.

An die Arbeit

Test yourself

Task 1

Steffi talks about jobs and her family. Match the people with the right jobs.

Vater
Mutter
Schwester
Bruder
Steffi

Task 2

Meike und Erdal besprechen ihr Arbeitspraktikum. Hör zu und füll die Lücken aus.

a) Erdal hat in einem ___ gearbeitet.

b) Meike hat in einer ___ gearbeitet.

c) Erdal musste fotokopieren, ___ ___ und Geschirr ___ .

d) Meike musste ___ helfen, Sport ___ und Geschichten ___ .

e) Erdal hat das Praktikum ___ und ___ gefunden.

f) Um Lehrer zu werden, muss man ___ sein.

Answers

Task 1
a) Bruder; b) Mutter; c) Steffi; d) Schwester; e) Vater.

Task 2
a) Büro; b) Schule; c) Kaffee machen; d) Kindern; treiben/machen; vorlesen; spülen/waschen; e) anstrengend; langweilig; f) geduldig.

German Revision Guide

Task 3

Conversation: use the Mind Map below to help you talk about work.

> **HIGHER LEVEL** Add *further study / training – why?* to the Mind Map.

Task 4

Du hast einen Samstagsjob in einem Geschäft. Schreib einen Bericht über deinen Job.

Sag ...wo du arbeitest;
...wie du zur Arbeit kommst;
...wie lange die Fahrt dauert;
...wie viele Stunden pro Tag du arbeitest;
...wie viel Geld du verdienst;
...wie du die Arbeit findest;

Task 5

Du bekommst einen Brief von einem deutschen Brieffreund. Er fragt über deine Zukunftspläne. In deiner Antwort musst du folgendes erwähnen:

– weitere Ausbildung (z.B. Abitur, Hochschule, Uni)

– Berufspläne – was du machen willst und warum

– andere Pläne (reisen, heiraten usw.)

Model answer

Task 4
Samstags arbeite ich in einem Supermarkt. Ich fahre mit dem Rad zur Arbeit. Die Fahrt dauert 10 Minuten. Ich arbeite sechs Stunden pro Tag und ich verdiene 2 Pfund 50 pro Stunde. Ich finde die Arbeit ziemlich langweilig.

Task 5
Hallo Hans! Hier sind meine Zukunftspläne! Nächstes Jahr bleibe ich hier auf der Schule. Ich werde Deutsch, Geschichte und Englisch in der Oberstufe lernen. Nach dem Abitur möchte ich auf die Uni gehen, um englische Literatur zu studieren. Ich will Lehrerin werden, denn ich arbeite gern mit Kindern und ich finde die Literatur sehr interessant.
Ich werde mit 21 Jahren eine Weltreise machen, denn ich reise sehr gern, und ich möchte mit 30 Jahren heiraten und vielleicht 2 oder 3 Kinder haben.

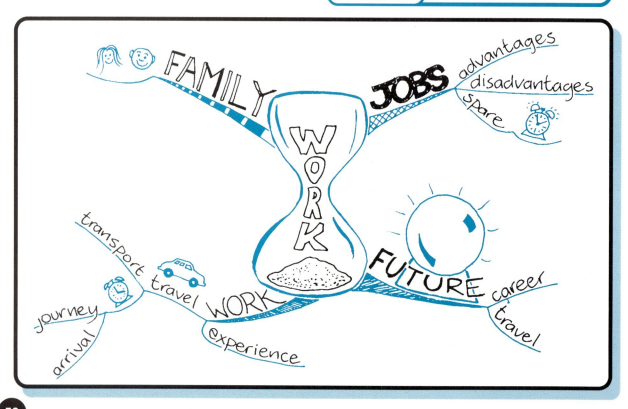

6 Die Stadt ruft

Market forces

It's Saturday morning, but for once Marlene would almost rather be at school. Großtante Maria has broken her leg in a motorbike accident, and both Müller parents have been summoned to her bedside. This means two unaccustomed and unwelcome extra duties for Marlene: babysitting for Martin and shopping at the local market.

Marlene is not impressed by her dad's shopping list. For one thing, it's too long, and for another, it's not properly organised. Look for yourself – Herr Müller has mixed fruit with meat, shampoo with cheese and bread with chocolate.

Einkaufsliste

Apfelsinen	Kekse	Quark
Rindfleisch	Möhren	Grüner Salat
Chips	Bonbons	Honig
Pfirsiche	Tomaten	Zucker
Zahnpasta	Apfelkuchen	Milch
Seife	Schweinefleisch	Waschpulver
Brötchen	Mehl	Haarwaschmittel
Erbsen	Hähnchen	Joghurt
Vollkornbrot	Kohl	Käse
Kartoffeln	Gurke	Spülmittel

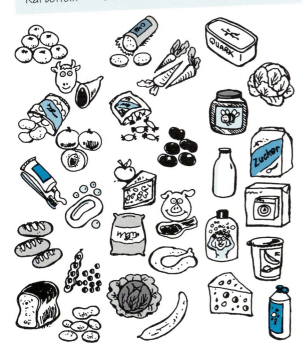

checklist

What would you ssy if you had to …

	Kein Problem!	Hilfe!

FOUNDATION LEVEL

- talk about your home town? ○ ○
- give and understand directions? ○ ○
- find out about opening and closing times? ○ ○
- ask about and buy things in shops? ○ ○
- say how you are feeling? ○ ○

HIGHER LEVEL

- find your way round a store? ○ ○
- talk about shopping? ○ ○
- take something back to a shop? ○ ○
- understand about special offers, reductions and sales? ○ ○
- talk to a doctor, dentist or chemist? ○ ○
- ask and answer questions about treatment? ○ ○

German Revision Guide

Oh well, thinks Marlene, why not kill three birds with one stone? Get Martin to rewrite the list, putting the items into groups according to which market stall they are to be found in. That will keep him busy for a while, make the shopping trip easier, and meanwhile she can have an extra quarter of an hour in the bath.

Five minutes later, Martin has made a start, but he would appreciate some help. Copy out the names of the stalls below and then finish the job for him by putting the items from the shopping list under the right heading. There are pictures to help you with the meanings.

An hour later, Marlene and Martin have arrived at the market in Kippenstadt and are systematically working their way round. By the time they get to the meat stall, Martin's patience is wearing thin and he is demanding compensation for having to waste his Saturday morning in this way.

Verkäufer	Bitte schön?
Marlene	Haben Sie Rindfleisch und Schweinefleisch?
Verkäufer	Ja, klar.
Marlene	Ein Kilo Rindfleisch und fünfhundert Gramm Schweinefleisch, bitte.
Verkäufer	Sonst noch etwas?
Marlene	Nein, das ist alles.
Martin	Doch! Ein Stück Wurst für mich. Ich habe Hunger!
Marlene	Okay, Martin. Was kostet das?
Verkäufer	Das macht einundzwanzig Mark fünfzig insgesamt.

Anything for a quiet life, thinks Marlene, and Martin gets his slice of sausage. But as they go round the market he asks for more and more. Using the **Wortautomat** and the **Einkaufsliste** to help you, write down the conversations they have at the other stalls, where Martin demands the following things:

<u>Bäckerei</u>: ein Sesambrötchen
<u>Konditorei</u>: Schokolade
<u>Obst und Gemüse</u>: eine Banane
<u>Lebensmittel</u>: Chips

Answers

Drogerie: Zahnpasta, Seife, Haarwaschmittel;
Konditorei: Bonbons, Apfelkuchen;
Metzgerei: Rindfleisch, Schweinefleisch, Hähnchen;
Bäckerei: Vollkornbrot, Brötchen;
Lebensmittel: Chips, Kekse, Mehl, Honig, Zucker;
Obst und Gemüse: Apfelsinen, Pfirsiche, Tomaten, Kartoffeln, Kohl, Möhren, Erbsen, Gurke, Grüner Salat;
Haushalt: Spülmittel, Waschpulver;
Milchprodukte: Quark, Milch, Joghurt, Käse

Die Stadt ruft

Wortautomat

Bitte schön?	**Can I help you?**
Ich möchte...	I'd like...
Haben Sie...?	**Have you got...?**
hundert Gramm Wurst	100 g sausage
fünfhundert Gramm Schweinefleisch	500 g pork
ein Pfund Tomaten	a pound of tomatoes
ein Liter Milch	a litre of milk
ein Kilo Rindfleisch	a kilo of beef
ein Stück Kuchen	a piece of cake
ein Päckchen Butter	a packet of butter
einen Becher Joghurt	a tub of yoghurt
ein Glas Honig	a jar of honey
eine Tube Zahnpasta	a tube of toothpaste
eine Schachtel Pralinen	a box of chocolates
eine Flasche Bier	a bottle of beer
eine Tafel Schokolade	a bar of chocolate
eine Tüte Bonbons	a bag of sweets
eine Dose Sardinen	a tin of sardines
Vollkornbrot	wholemeal bread
Wir haben (leider)	(Unfortunately) we have no
kein Schweinefleisch.	pork.
keine Wurst.	sausage.
kein Bier.	beer.
keine Bonbons.	sweets.
Sonst noch etwas?	**Anything else?**
Nein, das ist alles.	No, that's all.
Doch!* ...für mich!	Yes! ...for me!

(*Said when disagreeing with someone.*)

Ich habe Hunger / Durst.	I'm hungry / thirsty.
Was kostet das?	**How much does that cost?**
Das macht... (insgesamt).	That's... (all together).

By the time they've finished, Martin is not feeling too well...

Marlene	Martin! Du siehst schrecklich aus! Was ist los?
Martin	Ich habe Magenschmerzen.
Marlene	Dummkopf! Du hast zu viel gegessen!
Martin	Ich glaube, ich muss brechen.
Marlene	Wo ist die Apotheke?
Martin	Ich weiß es nicht.
Marlene	Entschuldigen Sie. Wo ist die nächste Apotheke?
Frau	Also, geht hier links, nehmt die erste Straße rechts und ihr seht eine große Apotheke an der linken Seite neben der Post. Aber beeilt euch. Sie schließt in zehn Minuten.
Marlene	Vielen Dank!

Imagine that you and a friend are out shopping in Germany when one of you suddenly starts to feel unwell. You decide that the best thing is to ask someone how to get to the nearest chemist. Using the **Wortautomat** and Marlene and Martin's conversation to help you, make up as many different versions of the conversation as you can think of in four minutes. Change at least one thing each time: the symptoms, the directions, how long before closing time.

Wortautomat

Du siehst... aus.	You look...
Was ist los?	**What's wrong?**
Wie geht's?	**How are you?**
Ich habe Magenschmerzen / Bauchschmerzen.	I've got a stomach ache.
Kopfschmerzen.	a headache.
Ohrenschmerzen.	ear ache.
Zahnschmerzen.	toothache.
Halsschmerzen.	a sore throat.
Rückenschmerzen.	backache.
Durchfall.	diarrhoea
Husten.	a cough.
Fieber.	a temperature.
Grippe.	the 'flu.
einen Schnupfen.	a cold.
Mein Bein / Arm / Fuß / Finger tut weh.	My leg / arm / finger hurts.
Meine Hand	hand
Ich bin krank.	I'm ill.
müde.	tired.
Mir ist kalt / heiß.	I'm hot / cold.
Ich glaube, ich muss brechen.	I think I'm going to be sick.
Dummkopf! Du hast zu viel gegessen!	Idiot! You've eaten too much!
Entschuldigung!	Excuse me!

Wo ist der nächste... **Where's the nearest...**
  Supermarkt / Zeitungskiosk / Markt?   **supermarket / newspaper kiosk / market?**
die nächste...   the nearest...
  Apotheke   **chemist's (pharmacy)**
  Bäckerei   **bakery**
  Drogerie   **chemist's (no medication)**
  Konditorei   **confectioner's**
  Post   **post office**
  Metzgerei   **butcher's**
  Bibliothek   **library**
  Buchhandlung?   **bookshop?**
das nächste...   the nearest...
  Kaufhaus / Verkehrsamt?   **department store / tourist office?**

i) Geh
ii) Geht   hier links / rechts / geradeaus.   Go left / right / straight on here.
iii) Gehen Sie*

Die Stadt ruft

i) Nimm	Take the first / second / third road on the right.
ii) Nehmt die erste / zweite / dritte Straße rechts	
iii) Nehmen Sie*	
i) du siehst	you'll see
ii) ihr seht	
iii) Sie sehen*	
an der linken / rechten Seite	on the left / right
neben der Post	next to the post office
gegenüber von	opposite
neben dem Supermarkt / Rathaus	next to the supermarket / town hall
gegenüber vom	opposite
i) Beeil dich	Hurry up
ii) Beeilt euch	
iii) Beeilen Sie sich*	

Wann schließt die Apotheke? — **When does the chemist's shut?**
Wann ist der Supermarkt geöffnet? — **When is the supermarket open?**
Er / Sie / Es schließt in zehn Minuten. — It shuts in 10 minutes.
         öffnet um 9 Uhr. —   opens at 9 o'clock.

*Remember that there are three different ways of saying 'you' in German:
i) is for when you talk to a friend or a member of your family;
ii) is for more than one friend / family member;
iii) is for when you speak to one or more adult you don't know very well.

Now swallow that!

Luckily, Marlene and Martin manage to get to the **Apotheke** just before closing time.

Marlene	Haben Sie etwas gegen Magenschmerzen für meinen Bruder?
Mann	Seit wann hast du Magenschmerzen?
Martin	Seit zehn Minuten. Ich habe zu viel gegessen.
Mann	Wenn es dir in einer halben Stunde nicht besser geht, kannst du dieses Mittel nehmen. Nimm einen Teelöffel alle vier Stunden. Wenn es dir in zwei Tagen nicht besser geht, dann gehst du am besten zum Arzt.
Martin	Schnell, Marlene! Ich muss dringend aufs Klo!

Just before the shop closes, four more people arrive. Each has a different problem. Imagine their conversations with the chemist:

1 cough / 1 week / cough mixture – 1tsp 2 × daily

2 flu / yesterday / tablets – 1 × evenings

3 toothache / 2 days / go to dentist

4 diarrhoea / this morning / medicine – 3 × daily before meals

German Revision Guide

Wortautomat

Haben Sie etwas gegen Magenschmerzen?	**Have you got anything for stomach ache?**
dagegen?	it?
Seit wann hast du / haben Sie das?	**How long have you had it?**
Seit zwei Tagen.	For two days.
heute morgen.	Since this morning.
gestern.	yesterday.
Wenn es dir in... nicht besser geht...	If you're not better in...
Du kannst / Sie können diesen Hustensaft	You can take this cough mixture.
dieses Mittel nehmen.	this medicine.
diese Tabletten	these tablets.
Nimm / Nehmen Sie einen / zwei Teelöffel	Take one / two teaspoons
eine Tablette	one tablet
alle... Stunden.	every... hours.
vor / nach den Mahlzeiten.	before / after meals.
morgens/abends.	in the morning / evening.
zweimal pro Tag.	twice a day.
Am besten gehst du / gehen Sie zum Arzt / Zahnarzt.	You'd better go to the doctor's / dentist's
Schnell! Ich muss (dringend) aufs Klo.	Quick! I need the loo (desperately).

Meanwhile, just a kilometre away, Gerhard and Gabi are cycling towards the town centre.

Gerhard Hier ist Kippenstadt, Gabi! Schön, oder?
Gabi Was ist schön?
Gerhard Also, im Park gibt es viele Bäume und Blumen und einen Teich mit Enten und Fischen. Im Stadtzentrum haben wir das alte Rathaus, den Markt und das große Einkaufszentrum. Es gibt auch das Freizeitzentrum, wo man viele verschiedene Sportarten treiben kann.

Gabi Die Stadt ist zwar ziemlich groß, schön finde ich sie aber nicht. Meine Stadt ist viel besser, obwohl sie sehr touristisch ist.
Gerhard Ja, das stimmt. Kippenstadt ist leider zu industriell. Ich würde lieber auf dem Land wohnen.
Gabi Auf dem Land! Das wäre so langweilig! Fahren wir jetzt zum Einkaufszentrum.
Gerhard Zuerst muss ich zur Post.

Wortautomat

Schön, oder?	**Nice, isn't it?**
Was gibt es in deiner Gegend?	**What is there in your area?**
Es gibt / Wir haben...	There is / We have...
einen Teich mit Enten und Fischen	a pond with ducks and fish
einen Dom	a cathedral
einen Park	a park

Die Stadt ruft

eine Kirche	a church
eine Polizeiwache	a police station
eine Brücke	a bridge
eine Burg	a castle
ein Rathaus	a town hall
ein Einkaufszentrum	a shopping centre
ein Freizeitzentrum	a leisure centre
ein Krankenhaus	a hospital
Bäume	trees
Blumen	flowers
…wo man viele verschiedene Sportarten treiben kann.	…where you can do lots of differents types of sport.
Fußball spielen kann.	play football.
spazieren gehen kann.	go for walks.

Wie ist deine Gegend?
Ich wohne in einer Kleinstadt/Großstadt.
    in einem Dorf.
    auf dem Land.

What's your area like?
I live in a small / large town.
    a village.
    the country.

Die Stadt ist zwar groß, aber…
obwohl sie sehr… ist
(→**obwohl**, like **weil**, *sends the verb to the end of the phrase.*)
touristisch
industriell
historisch
leider
Welche Stadt gefällt dir besser, X oder Y?
X ist (viel) größer / kleiner / schöner als Y.
Wohnst du gern in der Stadt / auf dem Land?
Ich würde lieber auf dem Land / in der Stadt wohnen.
Das wäre…

It's true the town is big, but…
although it's very…

touristy
industrial
historical
unfortunately
Which town do you prefer, X or Y?
X is larger / smaller / more beautiful than Y.
Do you like living in the town / country?
I'd rather live in the country / town.

That would be…

Now it's your turn to tell Gerhard about where you live. Remember to say whether you live in the town or the country, what sort of place it is, what there is to see, what you can do there, and whether you like living there.

High Street Blues

Gerhard and Gabi have now arrived at the post office, where Gerhard is stocking up on stamps for his letters to Tracy Turner and Gabi is having an attack of jealousy.

Gerhard	Was kostet eine Briefmarke für einen Brief nach Großbritannien?
Frau	Eine Mark.
Gerhard	Zehn Briefmarken zu einer Mark, bitte.
Gabi	Wie viele englische Brieffreundinnen hast du eigentlich?
Gerhard	Nur eine.

What will Gerhard say when he wants to send Tracy
a) a postcard,
b) a birthday present?

German Revision Guide

 Heading towards the **Einkaufszentrum**, Gabi is quick to forget about Gerhard's international love life. Shopping is her obsession, and she allows nothing to detract from her enjoyment of it. Here's what she has to say on the subject:

Ich gehe sehr gern einkaufen. Fast jeden Samstag fahren meine Schwester und ich mit dem Bus in die Stadt. Manchmal machen wir einen Schaufensterbummel. Aber wenn ich genug Geld habe, gehe ich in meine Lieblingsboutique, *Klick*. *Klick* ist toll – es gibt immer die neueste Mode. Wir probieren alles an. Es macht viel Spaß. Die Verkäuferinnenn sind sehr hilfsbereit. Normalerweise kaufe ich etwas Schönes für die Disco – vielleicht einen Minirock oder ein Kleid. Letzten Samstag habe ich eine tolle Bluse aus Seide gekauft.

Oft essen wir zu Mittag in einem italienischen Restaurant. Um sechzehn Uhr fahren wir mit dem Taxi nach Hause. Danach bin ich immer total kaputt!

Wortautomat

Was kostet eine Briefmarke für einen Brief nach...?	How much is a stamp for a letter to...?
eine Postkarte	postcard
Ich möchte dieses Päckchen nach... schicken.	I'd like to send this parcel to...
Eine Briefmarke zu einer Mark, bitte.	A 1-Mark stamp, please.
Zwei Briefmarken zwei	Two 2-Mark stamps,
eigentlich	actually
nur	only
fast	almost
Manchmal machen wir einen Schaufensterbummel.	Sometimes we go window shopping.
Wenn ich genug Geld habe,	If I have enough money,
meine Lieblingsboutique	my favourite clothes shop
mein Lieblingsgeschäft	my favourite shop
die neueste Mode	the latest fashions
billig / teuer	cheap / expensive
Wir probieren alles an.	We try everything on.
etwas Schönes	something nice
vielleicht	perhaps
Letzten Samstag habe ich... gekauft.	Last Saturday I bought...
aus Seide / Leder / Baumwolle / Wolle	made of silk / leather / cotton / wool
Oft essen wir zu Mittag in	We often have lunch in
einem italienischen Restaurant.	an Italian restaurant.
chinesischen	a Chinese
indischen	an Indian
im Schnellimbiss.	a burger bar.
danach	afterwards
immer	always
total kaputt	shattered

Die Stadt ruft

Gabi would like to know how you feel about shopping for clothes. How well can you answer her questions?
- Gehst du gern einkaufen?
- Wie kommst du in die Stadt? Mit wem?
- Was ist dein Lieblingsgeschäft? Warum?
- Was kaufst du normalerweise?
- Was hast du letztes Wochenende gekauft?
- Wo isst du in der Stadt zu Mittag?
- Um wie viel Uhr kommst du nach Hause?

Gerhard and Gabi have just arrived at **Kaufparadies**, a large department store in the **Einkaufszentrum**. Gabi's eye has been caught by a large notice in the window:

What does it say?

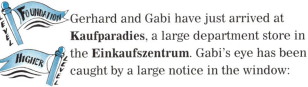

Answers: Only this week – special offer in Ladies' department – 25% off summer fashion.

Once inside, Gabi is anxious to investigate.

Gabi	Wo ist die Damenabteilung?
Gerhard	Im ersten Stock.
Gabi	Gehen wir die Rolltreppe hinauf... Wie findest du diesen Minirock, Gerhard?
Gerhard	Schrecklich! Leder gefällt mir nicht.
Gabi	Ich finde ihn toll... Entschuldigung! Kann ich das anprobieren?
Assistentin	Ja klar. Die Kabinen sind dort drüben.

Fünf Minuten später.

Gabi	Ich glaube, der Rock ist mir zu groß.
Assistentin	Möchten Sie eine Nummer kleiner?
Gabi	Ja, bitte... Viel besser! Ich nehme ihn! Kann ich diese Hose anprobieren?

Gabi tries on the following things, none of which Gerhard likes:
einen langen blauen Mantel
eine grüne Jacke
ein gelbes Hemd
weiße Schuhe.

Using the **Wortautomat** to help you, imagine the conversations.

Wortautomat

Wo ist die Damenabteilung?
    die Herrenabteilung?
Im Untergeschoss.
   Erdgeschoss.
   ersten / zweiten Stock.
Gehen wir die Rolltreppe hinauf.
           Treppe   hinunter.
Fahren wir mit dem Fahrstuhl.

Wie findest du diesen Rock?
          diese Bluse?
          dieses Hemd?
          diese Schuhe?
Ich finde ihn / sie / es / sie...

Where is the ladieswear department?
          menswear
In the basement.
On the ground floor.
   the first / second floor.
Let's go up   the escalator.
            down the stairs.
Let's take the lift.

What do you think of this skirt?
              blouse?
              shirt?
              these shoes?
I find it / them...

German Revision Guide

Kann ich das anprobieren?
Die Kabinen sind dort drüben.
Der Rock ist mir zu groß
              klein
              eng
              weit
              kurz
              lang.
Die Farbe gefällt mir (nicht).

Welche Größe?
eine Nummer größer / kleiner
Ich nehme ihn / sie / es / sie (nicht).

Can I try it on?
The changing rooms are over there.
The skirt is too big
            small
            narrow
            loose
            short
            long   for me.
I (don't) like the colour.

What size?
A size larger / smaller.
I'll (not) take it / them.

As Gabi tries on more and more outfits, Gerhard's patience begins to wear thin. He finally walks out of the shop while she is trying on some particularly tasteless fur-lined boots. That's it, he thinks – it's over. He wonders what he ever saw in her. In any case, he has other things to do. He's got a Saturday job at the leisure centre snack bar and he starts at 2 o'clock...

TAKE A BREAK

Test yourself

Task 1

Roleplay: You are in a food shop and want to buy some things for a picnic.

Bitte schön?

a)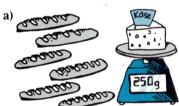

Sonst noch etwas?

b)

Ja. Ist das alles?

c)

Das macht 9 Mark 50 insgesamt.

Task 2

You are at the doctor's with a bad stomach upset. Tell the doctor what is wrong, how long you've been ill, and ask if he / she can give you anything for it. Finally, ask where the nearest chemist's is.

Die Stadt ruft

Task 3

Conversation: Use the Mind Map below to help you to talk about your local area.

 Add *opinions* and *comparisons with other areas* to the Mind Map.

Task 4

An der Tür eines Supermarktes:

	auf	zu
Werktags	0900	1230
	1300	1800
Samstags	0930	1400
Sonntags	—	—

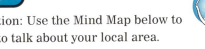

Richtig ✓ oder falsch ✗?

a) Der Supermarkt ist jeden Tag außer sonntags geöffnet.
b) Dienstags schließt er um 6 Uhr.
c) Die Mittagspause dauert eine Stunde.

Answers

Task 1
a) Sechs Brötchen, zweihundertfünfzig Gramm Käse und eine Tüte Chips
b) Haben Sie (eine Flasche) Limonade?
c) Ja. Was kostet das?

Task 2
Ich habe Magenschmerzen / Bauchschmerzen
Ich bin krank seit zwei Tagen / seit Samstag.
Haben Sie etwas dagegen?
Wo ist die nächste Apotheke?

Task 4 a) ✓ b) ✓ c) ✗

Freizeit macht Spaß!

7

checklist

What would you say if you had to ...

	Kein Problem!	Hilfe!
ask for permission to do things?	●	●
talk about times and ideas for going out?	●	●
ask for and give times and prices of activities?	●	●
buy tickets for activities?	●	●
say which foods you like / dislike?	●	●
ask for things in a restaurant or café?	●	●
find out what's on at the cinema or theatre?	●	●
say what you thought of a show?	●	●
HIGHER LEVEL		
report a loss or theft?	●	●
talk about watching or playing different sports?	●	●
ask for a little more to eat or drink or say you have enough?	●	●
say how many there are in a group?	●	●
ask for a table?	●	●
say where you would like to sit?	●	●
make a complaint, saying why?	●	●
ask about service charges?	●	●

Persuasion

It's late morning and Martin and Marlene are back at home. Marlene has unpacked the shopping, sent Martin to bed, and is planning her afternoon's entertainment. Unfortunately, Martin seems to have made a miraculous recovery and is now making unwelcome demands on her time.

Martin Ich langweile mich. Ich will ausgehen.
Marlene Du darfst nicht. Du bist krank. Du sollst im Bett bleiben und deine Tabletten nehmen.
Martin Nein! Jetzt geht's mir besser. Marlene, bitte. Darf ich ins Schwimmbad gehen? Du kannst mitkommen.
Marlene Ich bleibe lieber zu Hause, Martin. Ich wollte heute nachmittag fernsehen.
Martin Weißt du, Marlene, Gerhard Grün hat einen Samstagsjob im Freizeitzentrum...

Martin is used to this sort of conversation as people are always trying to stop him from doing what he wants to do, though somehow he usually ends up getting his own way.

Working with a friend, act out the following conversations which took place between Martin and his mother or father last week:

- Martin wants to go the cinema, but he's not allowed to as he's supposed to be doing his homework.
- He wants to go out with his friends but he's told he's got to do the washing up.
- He'd like to go into town with his mum / dad but s/he says s/he wanted to go to the park.

Freizeit macht Spaß!

Wortautomat

Ich langweile mich.		I'm bored.	
Darf ich...?	(mit meinen / deinen Freunden) ausgehen.	Can I...?	go out (with my / your friends)
Du darfst (nicht)	schwimmen gehen.	You can('t)	go swimming.
Ich will	zum Park gehen.	I want to	go to the park.
Ich wollte	ins Kino / Konzert / Freizeitzentrum gehen.	I wanted to	go to the cinema / concert / leisure centre.
Ich möchte	in die Stadt gehen.	I'd like to	go into town.
Du sollst	fernsehen.	You're supposed to	watch TV.
Du mußt	im Bett / zu Hause bleiben.	You must	stay in bed / at home.
Du kannst	Tabletten nehmen.	You can	take tablets.
	deine Hausaufgaben machen.		do your homework.
	mitkommen.		come too.
lieber		rather	
Weißt du...?		**Do you know...?**	

Fortunately for Martin, Marlene decides that she would quite like to go to the leisure centre after all, but first of all, she rings up to check when it's open.

You ring up a leisure centre in Germany to find out the following information. Write down the conversation:

Marlene	Um wie viel Uhr hat das Schwimmbad heute auf?
Empfangsdame	Heute nachmittag von 14 bis 18 Uhr.
Marlene	Und was kostet es?
Empfangsdame	5 Mark für Erwachsene und 2 Mark 50 für Kinder unter 14.
Marlene	Vielen Dank. Auf Wiederhören!

- Do they have an outdoor swimming-pool and how much does it cost for an adult and a child?
- Is it open on Sundays?
- Do they have any badminton courts for Saturday afternoon?
- Can you reserve a court for 4.30 p.m. for half an hour?

Wortautomat

Um wie viel Uhr hat / macht das Schwimmbad auf?
                         das Sportzentrum zu?
Hat das Schwimmbad freitags auf?
Heute morgen / nachmittag von... bis...
Morgen früh
Was kostet es für Erwachsene / Kinder?
Haben Sie Tennis- / Federball- / Squashplätze
          ein Hallenbad / ein Freibad?
Wann können wir spielen?
Ich möchte einen Federballplatz für 10 Uhr für
   eine (halbe) Stunde reservieren.

What time is / does the swimming-pool open?
                 sport centre   close?
Is the swimming-pool open on Fridays?
This morning / afternoon from... to...
Tomorrow morning
How much is it for adults / children?
Have you got any tennis / badminton / squash courts?
          an indoor / outdoor pool?
When can we play?
I'd like to book a badminton court for 10 o'clock
   for (half) an hour.

Gibt es eine Ermäßigung für Kinder / Studenten / Arbeitslose / Rentner?

Is there a reduction for children / students / unemployed / pensioners?

7

German Revision Guide

Men in tights

Marlene and Martin arrive at the **Kippenstadter Freizeitzentrum** at 2 o'clock, but when they try to buy a ticket for Martin to swim, they are interrupted by a woman who believes that she has been robbed.

Martin	Einmal schwimmen, bitte.
Frau	Entschuldigen Sie! Meine Handtasche ist gestohlen worden! Alles war dadrin!
Empfangsdame	Sind Sie sicher?
Frau	Rufen Sie die Polizei sofort an!
Empfangsdame	Moment, bitte. Wie sieht Ihre Tasche aus?
Frau	Sie ist aus Leder und ziemlich klein und braun. Mein Geldbeutel mit meiner Kreditkarte und hundert Mark war darin.
Empfangsdame	Wie ist Ihr Name, bitte?
Frau	Fisch, Franziska Fisch. Warum rufen Sie die Polizei nicht an?
Empfangsdame	Frau Fisch, hier ist Ihre Tasche. Sie haben das im Café vergessen...

You are at the leisure centre and have lost your wallet and passport. Explain what has happened to the receptionist, giving a description of the wallet and its contents. As your things have not been found, ask the receptionist to call the police.

Wortautomat

Einmal / zweimal schwimmen.	One / Two (tickets) to swim.
Meine Tasche ist gestohlen worden.	My bag has been stolen.
Meine Brieftasche	My wallet
Mein Geldbeutel	My purse
Mein Pass	My passport
Ich habe meinen Regenschirm verloren. / meine Handtasche	I've lost my umbrella / handbag.
Hast du gefunden?	**Have you found...?**
Haben Sie gesehen?	**Have you seen?**
darin	inside
sicher	sure
Rufen Sie die Polizei sofort an!	Call the police immediately!
Sie haben das im Café vergessen.	You left it in the café.
Ich habe in den Toiletten	I in the toilets.
Es tut mir Leid, wir haben Ihren Regenschirm / Ihre Handtasche nicht.	I'm sorry, we haven't got your umbrella / handbag.
Am besten gehen Sie zum Fundbüro.	You'd better go to the lost property office.

Freizeit macht Spaß!

Brief encounter

Upstairs in the **Iss-Dich-Fit Café**, Gerhard has started his afternoon shift and is trying to promote some of the healthier options on the menu. But the couple he is serving are relieved to find that other snacks are also available.

Iss-Dich-Fit Café

Zu essen	Preis
Gemischter Salat	DM 6,50
Gemüsesuppe	DM 7,00
Linsenpastete mit Vollkornbrot und Tomaten	DM 10,00
Hähnchen oder Bockwurst mit Pommes frites	DM 4,50

Zu trinken	
Mineralwasser	DM 6,00
Orangensaft	DM 7,50
Kräutertee	DM 3,00
Tee	DM 2,50
Kaffee mit oder ohne Koffein	DM 2,50
Sahne	DM 1,00

Bedienung einbegriffen

Frau	Entschuldigung!
Gerhard	Bitte schön?
Frau	Was haben Sie zu trinken?
Gerhard	Kräutertee, Mineralwasser, Orangensaft…
Mann	Gibt's keinen Kaffee?
Gerhard	Doch. Das haben wir auch. Mit oder ohne Koffein.
Frau	Und zu essen?
Gerhard	Gemüsesuppe oder Linsenpastete mit Vollkornbrot.
Mann	Ich esse nicht gern Gemüse. Ist das alles?
Gerhard	Nein. Wir haben auch Pommes mit Hähnchen oder Bockwurst.
Frau	Also, zweimal Kaffee mit Koffein, und zweimal Pommes mit Bockwurst. Bringen Sie bitte Senf und Ketchup.

What would you choose from the **Iss-Dich-Fit** menu? Imagine that you are very hungry and thirsty after two hours of hard exercise and that Gerhard is trying to persuade you to have something healthy. Do you give in, or go for the chips? Write down the conversation.

Wortautomat

Was haben Sie zu trinken / essen?	**What do you have to drink / eat?**
Gibt's (keinen) Kaffee?	**Is there (no) coffee?**
Kräutertee	herbal tea
mit oder ohne Koffein	with or without caffein
Milch	milk
Sahne	cream
Zucker	sugar
einmal / zweimal Kaffee	coffee for one / two
Gemüsesuppe	vegetable soup
Ich esse / trinke (nicht) gern…	I (don't) like eating / drinking…
Pommes	chips
Hähnchen	chicken
Bockwurst	type of sausage
Hamburger	beefburger
ein Hot Dog	a hot dog
mit Zwiebeln	with onions
Bringen Sie bitte…	Please bring…
Senf / Ketchup / Salz / Pfeffer / Essig	some mustard / ketchup / salt / pepper / vinegar
die Speisekarte / Karte	the menu
das Menü	fixed price menu
Was ist genau…?	**What is… exactly?**
Das war lecker / zu salzig / zu süß / ekelhaft!	That was delicious / too salty / too sweet / disgusting!
Wo sind die Toiletten?	**Where are the toilets?**
Zahlen, bitte.	The bill, please.

As Gerhard returns from the kitchen with a tray of frighteningly unhealthy food, he notices a familiar figure sitting in the corner, trying not to look in his direction…

7
German Revision Guide

Gerhard	Marlene. Hallo.
Marlene	Gerhard! Ich wusste nicht...
Gerhard	Möchtest du etwas zu trinken?
Marlene	Ja. Kaffee und... Gemüsesuppe.
Gerhard	Gemüsesuppe...? Ja, die Suppe ist heute sehr gut...
Marlene	Ich bin hier mit Martin. Er schwimmt gern. Ich schaue lieber zu. Du treibst viel Sport, oder?
Gerhard	Ziemlich viel. Am liebsten spiele ich Federball. Hast du das je gespielt?
Marlene	Nein, aber ich möchte es lernen. Spielst du oft?
Gerhard	Letzte Woche habe ich in einem Turnier gespielt und ich habe fast gewonnen.
Marlene	Prima!

You are discussing sport with two German friends. Imagine that you all like different sports, and one of you prefers to watch rather than play. Try to get them interested in your favourite sport by asking them if they have ever tried it. Use as many expressions from the **Wortautomat** as you can.

Wortautomat

Ich wusste nicht.	I didn't know.
Möchtest du / Möchten Sie...?	**Would you like...?**
Treibst du gern Sport?	**Do you like doing sport?**
Spielst du oder schaust du lieber zu?	**Do you prefer to play or watch?**
Ich schaue lieber zu.	I prefer to watch.
Ich spiele lieber.	I prefer to play.
Ich schaue gern beim Fußball zu.	I like watching football.
Ich gehe jeden Samstag ins Stadion.	I go to the stadium every Saturday.
Hast du je... gespielt?	**Have you ever played...?**
Ja, ich spiele oft.	Yes, I play often.
Ja, aber ich habe nur einmal gespielt.	Yes, but I've only played once.
Es hat mir nicht gefallen.	I didn't like it.
Es hat Spaß gemacht.	It was fun.
Nein, ich habe keine Lust dazu.	No, I don't want to.
Nein, aber ich möchte es lernen.	No, but I'd like to learn it.
ein Turnier	a tournament
Ich habe (fast) gewonnen / verloren.	I (nearly) won / lost.

After his brief conversation with Marlene, Gerhard goes off to the kitchen to prepare her coffee and soup. It's very hot in there and he has to sit down for a moment. It seems impossible that they have spoken – after all these years of ignoring each other! But they were children then.

When Gerhard returns to the table, Marlene asks him to join her for a while, as there are no other customers.

Marlene	Sag mal... ist Gabi auch hier?
Gerhard	Nein. Eigentlich gehen wir nicht mehr miteinander aus.
Marlene	Was ist passiert?
Gerhard	Ich finde sie langweilig und selbstsüchtig. Sie ist zwar schön, aber das ist nicht genug.
Marlene	Was machst du heute abend?
Gerhard	Nichts besonderes. Warum?
Marlene	Hättest du Lust, heute abend ins Kino zu gehen?

Freizeit macht Spaß!

Gerhard	Was läuft?
Marlene	*Berliner Werwolf II* – hast du das schon gesehen?
Gerhard	Noch nicht. Ja, das wäre toll. Um wie viel Uhr beginnt der Film?
Marlene	Es gibt eine Vorstellung um sieben Uhr. Treffen wir uns um Viertel vor sieben vor dem Kino.
Gerhard	Ja, Okay. Fahren wir nicht mit dem Rad dahin?
Marlene	Ich fahre mit dem Bus. Du kannst mitfahren, wenn du willst.
Gerhard	Bis später, also!

You are organising an evening with some German friends. You have to decide what you'd like to do, where you're going, where and what time you're meeting, how you're getting there. Make the conversation as lively as you can, using lots of different expressions from the **Wortautomat**.

Wortautomat

Sag mal	Tell me
eigentlich	actually
Wir gehen (nicht mehr) miteinander aus.	We're (not) going out with each other (any more).
Was ist passiert?	**What happened?**
selbstsüchtig	selfish
Sie ist zwar schön	It's true she's good-looking.
genug	enough
Was machst du heute abend?	**What are you doing this evening?**
morgen?	**tomorrow?**
übermorgen?	**the day after tomorrow?**
am Samstag?	**on Saturday?**
Nichts (besonderes).	Nothing (in particular).
Ich gehe (schon) mit Karl aus.	I'm (already) going out with Karl.
Ich muss meine Hausaufgaben machen.	I have to do my homework.
meine Großmutter besuchen.	visit my Grandma.
auf meinen kleinen Bruder / meine klein Schwester aufpassen.	look after my little brother / sister.
Hättest du Lust, (heute abend) ins Kino zu gehen?	Do you fancy going to the cinema (this evening)?
schwimmen	swimming
Was läuft?	**What's on?**
Hast du das schon gesehen?	**Have you seen it already?**
Noch nicht.	Not yet.
Ja, das habe ich letzte Woche (mit meiner Schwester) gesehen.	Yes, I saw it last week (with my sister).
Das wäre toll / eine gute Idee.	That would be great / a good idea.
Wann beginnt / endet der Film?	When does the film start / end?
eine Vorstellung	a showing
Wo treffen wir uns?	Where shall we meet?
Wann	When
Um wie viel Uhr	What time

German Revision Guide

Treffen wir uns um... Uhr vor dem Kino / Sportplatz.
　　　　　　　　　　an der Bushaltestelle / U-Bahn.
　　　　　　　　　　am Bahnhof.
　　　　　　　　　　bei mir / dir / Hans.
Fahren wir (nicht) mit dem Rad / Auto / Bus dahin?
mitfahren
Bis später!

Let's meet at... o'clock in front of the cinema / sports centre.
　　　　　　　　　at the bus stop / underground.
　　　　　　　　　at the station.
　　　　　　　　　at my / your / Hans's house.
Are(n't) we going there by bike / car / bus?
to come too
See you later!

Dating the enemy

Later that evening, Marlene and Gerhard are coming out of the cinema talking about the film. It was supposed to be a horror film, but neither of them were very frightened by it.

Gerhard	Wie hast du das gefunden?
Marlene	Sehr komisch. Ich habe so viel gelacht.
Gerhard	Aber Claudia Nagel ist eine schlechte Schauspielerin.
Marlene	Sie ist doch lustig. Gefällt dir Theo Strack?
Gerhard	Der Werwolf? Ja. Er war aber nicht sehr schreckenerregend.
Marlene	Es war traurig, als er gestorben ist. Ich habe geweint. Er war süß.
Gerhard	Ein süßer Werwolf! Das ist doof.
Marlene	Ich habe Hunger. Gehen wir ins Restaurant.

Marlene would like to know about the last film you saw. Answer her questions as fully as you can.
• Welchen Film hast du gesehen?
• Wie hast du den Film gefunden?
• Warum?

Now tell her about a play or a concert you've been to.

Wortautomat

Wie hast du den Film?
　　　　　　　das Theaterstück gefunden?
　　　　　　　das Konzert?
lustig / komisch
traurig
interessant
langweilig
doof
schreckenerregend
spannend
Das finde ich auch.
Ich habe　　viel gelacht.
Wir haben　geweint.
Es hat viel Spaß gemacht.
eine gute schlechte Schauspielerin / Sängerin
ein guter / schlechter Schauspieler / Sänger
als er gestorben ist

What did you think of the film?
　　　　　　　　　　　　play?
　　　　　　　　　　　　concert?
funny
sad
interesting
boring
stupid
frightening
exciting
I agree.
I　　laughed a lot.
We　cried.
It was really good fun.
a good / bad actress / (female) singer
a good / bad actor / (male) singer
when he died

Finding the right place to eat isn't an easy task, but in the end Marlene persuades Gerhard to try the local Italian, *Il Cucchiaio*, where she can have plenty of garlic bread, and pizza, and he can order a large crispy salad.

Im Restaurant
Kellnerin Guten Abend. Haben Sie reserviert?
Marlene Nein. Haben Sie einen Tisch für zwei Personen?
Kellnerin Setzen Sie sich bitte hier.
Gerhard Lieber nicht neben den Toiletten. Können wir neben dem Fenster sitzen?

Am Tisch
Gerhard Was möchtest du?
Marlene Als Vorspeise möchte ich Knoblauchbrot. Und zum Hauptgericht esse ich Salamipizza. Und du?
Gerhard Ich nehme Melone und dann einen Tomatensalat mit Oliven.
Marlene Tomatensalat? Du spinnst wohl!
Gerhard Das schmeckt mir gut. Außerdem kann ich keine Pizza und kein Fleisch essen, denn ich bin Vegetarier und allergisch gegen Mozzarella.

20 Minuten später...
Marlene Entschuldigung! Wir warten seit 20 Minuten und haben noch nicht bestellt!
Kellnerin Es tut mir Leid. Ich habe Sie völlig vergessen. Was möchten Sie?

Das Hauptgericht
Gerhard Reich mir bitte den Pfeffer. Dieser Salat schmeckt nach nichts.
Marlene Und die Pizza ist zu kalt. Fräulein! Können Sie bitte diese Pizza aufwärmen?

Der Nachtisch
Kellnerin Was möchten Sie zum Nachtisch?
Gerhard Was ist genau *zuppa inglese*?
Kellnerin Das ist englische Suppe.
Marlene Nein, das stimmt nicht! Es ist eine Art von schlabberigem Kuchen.
Gerhard Nehmen wir Kaffee.

Die Rechnung
Kellnerin Noch etwas Kaffee?
Gerhard Nein, wir möchten bitte zahlen.
...
Marlene Sieh dir die Rechnung an! 900 Mark!
Gerhard Ist die Bedienung inbegriffen?
Marlene Nein!
Gerhard Fräulein! Die Rechnung ist falsch! 900 Mark!
Kellnerin Sie haben doch ziemlich viel gegessen.
Marlene Holen Sie den Koch!
Gerhard Den Koch? Ich will mit dem Geschäftsführer sprechen!

How well could you manage in a German restaurant? Practise the following situation with a friend playing the role of the waiter or waitress:
- ask for a table for three, outside
- ask for the menu, and order drinks
- order starters and main course
- ask someone to pass the salt
- make some sort of complaint about the food or service
- order a dessert, ask for the bill
- say that the bill is wrong and that you'd like to speak to the manager.

Wortautomat / Word bank

Haben Sie reserviert?	Have you reserved?
Haben Sie einen Tisch für... Personen?	Have you got a table for...?
Wir sind vier.	There are four of us.
lieber nicht	preferably not
neben dem Fenster	next to the window
draußen	outside

German Revision Guide

als Vorspeise	as a starter
zum Hauptgericht	as a main course
zum Nachtisch	for dessert
Knoblauchbrot	garlic bread
Ich nehme...	I'll have...
Du spinnst wohl!	You're mad!
Das schmeckt mir (nicht).	It tastes (doesn't taste) good to me.
außerdem	anyway
Ich kann keine Pizza essen.	I can't eat pizza.
kein Fleisch	meat.
Ich bin Vegetarier(in).	I'm a vegetarian.
Ich bin allergisch gegen...	I'm allergic to...
Wir warten seit... Minuten.	We've been waiting for... minutes.
Wir haben (noch nicht) bestellt.	We have(n't yet) ordered.
Ich habe Pizza bestellt.	I ordered pizza.
Es tut mir Leid.	I'm sorry.
völlig	completely
Reich mir bitte den Pfeffer / das Salz.	Pass me the pepper / salt, please.
Reichen Sie	
schmeckt nach nichts	is tasteless
nicht gekocht	not cooked
aufwärmen	warm up
etwas länger kochen	cook for a bit longer
eine Art von schlabberigem Kuchen	a sort of sloppy cake
Nehmen wir...	Let's have...
die Rechnung	the bill
Noch etwas Kaffee?	**Any more coffee?**
Wir möchten bitte zahlen.	We'd like to pay, please.
Ist die Bedienung einbegriffen?	**Is the service included?**
Holen Sie den Koch!	Get the cook!
mit dem Geschäftsführer sprechen	speak to the manager

To Gerhard's surprise, the cook turns out to be Marlene's dad, who gets very angry when Marlene complains about the quality of the food. But he does rip up the bill, so they get a free meal out of it. And at the end of the evening, Gerhard reckons he's had much more fun than he ever did with Gabi... Maybe there is more to life than vegetables and violins.

Test Yourself

Task 1

Du rufst im Kino an. Hör die Kassette an.

Richtig (✓) oder falsch (✗)?

a) Der Film heißt *Superman*.

b) Die erste Vorstellung beginnt um halb fünf.

c) Eine Karte für einen 16jährigen Jungen kostet 15 Mark.

Answers

Task 1
a) ✗ b) ✓ c) ✓

Freizeit macht Spaß!

Task 2

HIGHER LEVEL — Elke isst zu Mittag im Restaurant. Hör die Kassette an und beantworte die Fragen.

a) Was hatte zu viel Salz?
b) Was für Wein hat Elke bestellt?
c) Was wurde zu lange gekocht?
d) Was war nicht sehr warm?
e) Was war falsch?
f) Mit wem will Elke sprechen?

Task 3

Roleplay: To use this Mind Map you will need either to work with a friend, or play several different roles yourself. Imagine that you and your friend are planning an evening out. You'd like to go to the cinema or some sort of show and then on to a restaurant. Work out what you would say at each stage of the evening. Ask your friend to be the other person in each situation (parent, friend, ticket seller, waiter), and then swap roles.

HIGHER LEVEL — When you act out the restaurant scene, include the following:
- asking for a table for two
- saying where you would like to sit
- making a complaint
- asking about service charges.

Task 4

Im Freizeitzentrum

a)
Empfangsdame
Ja. Wann möchten Sie spielen?

b)
Empfangsdame
Ja, das geht. Wie lange möchten Sie spielen?

c)
Empfangsdame
Wollen Sie jetzt bezahlen?

d)
Empfangsdame
DM 16.

Answers

Task 2
a) die Tomatensuppe; b) eine halbe Flasche Weißwein; c) das Schnitzel; d) die Pommes (frites); e) die Rechnung; f) mit dem Geschäftsführer.

Task 4
a) Haben Sie (hier) Badmintonplätze? b) Am Freitag um 16 Uhr 30 / halb fünf. c) Eine Stunde / bis 17 Uhr 30. d) Was kostet es?

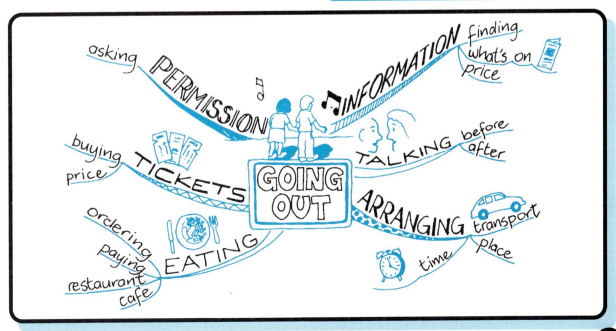

Los geht's!

checklist

What would you say if you had to ...

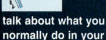

	Kein Problem!	Hilfe!
talk about what you normally do in your holidays?	●	●
say what you plan for your next holidays?	●	●
say what you did in your last holidays?	●	●
book different types of accommodation?	●	●
understand simple weather forecasts?	●	●
say what the weather is like?	●	●
buy tickets and find out information about public transport?	●	●

	Kein Problem!	Hilfe!
talk about what you prefer to do in the holidays and why?	●	●
say what other people do in the holidays?	●	●
talk and understand about the weather?	●	●
buy fuel at a petrol station?	●	●
talk and understand about car breakdown?	●	●
understand and talk about road accidents?	●	●

Different strokes

Summer is coming, and everyone's thinking about where to go for their holidays. Of course, the Grüns and the Müllers have very different ideas of how to enjoy themselves. For the Grüns, fresh air, walking and cycling come high up on the list, whereas the Müllers like to go somewhere hot and do as little as possible. This is fine, except that Marlene and Gerhard would now like to go on holiday together. The others think they're mad.

Here's what Gretchen and Marlene have to say about their holidays:

Gretchen ❛In den Sommerferien fahre ich normalerweise mit meiner Mutter und meinem Bruder aufs Land oder ans Meer. Wir fahren mit dem Zug und dem Rad und übernachten in Jugendherbergen oder auf Campingplätzen. Das finde ich toll, denn es ist sehr billig und ich finde viele neue Freunde aus verschiedenen Ländern: Schweizer, Engländer, Franzosen, usw.

Es gibt nur ein Problem: Das Essen. In den Jugendherbergen gibt es wenig für Vegetarier! Wir essen also viele Käsebrote – sehr langweilig. Meistens verbringen wir drei Wochen im Urlaub. Es macht Spaß! Jeden Tag machen wir Ausflüge: Wir wandern in den Bergen, schwimmen, fahren Rad, spielen

Tennis, tanzen, und besichtigen Burgen und Schlösser. '

Marlene 'Ich fahre am liebsten nach Spanien. Natürlich fliegen wir dahin – das ist viel schneller. Das Wetter ist schön und heiß und ich kann den ganzen Tag in der Sonne liegen, um braun zu werden.

Morgens stehe ich spät auf und gehe direkt zum Strandcafé, wo ich ,,churros" (Berliner) mit Schokolade esse. Meine Eltern sind schon seit eineinhalb Stunden am Strand, und Martin schwimmt im Meer.

Gegen 12 Uhr gehen wir ins Restaurant. Ich esse oft Fisch und Pommes. (Es gibt dort eine Menge Engländer.)

Nachmittags mache ich Siesta bis 16 Uhr, und dann bin ich noch zwei Stunden am Strand.

Abends gibt es viel zu tun. Man kann einkaufen gehen, tanzen, essen, trinken, plaudern usw. Ich gehe sehr gern in die Disco. Es gibt immer viele hübsche Jungs. Man kann die ganze Nacht tanzen. Wenn wir nach Hause fahren, bin ich immer sehr traurig. '

Gretchen and Marlene would now like to know about your holidays. Using their descriptions and the **Wortautomat** to help you, write as much as you can about where you go and what you do. Feel free to use your imagination – as long as you've got your story straight before you go in, the examiner is not going to know (or care) whether you are telling the truth.

As well as talking about where you normally go, you need to be ready to say where you will be going (in the future) and where you have been (in the past). The future is very easy, because you can use the present tense as long as you start off with a *time marker*, e.g.

Diesen Sommer fahre ich mit meinen Eltern nach Amerika.
This summer I'm going to America with my parents. (See the **Wortautomat** for other *time markers*).

Spend a few minutes practising talking about what you plan to do for the next holidays. If you're feeling lazy, it can be almost exactly the same as what you said you normally do.

If you want to really impress, use the future tense, which is actually quite easy. All you do is use **werden** *and the infinitive of the verb, e.g.*

Diesen Sommer **werde ich** mit meinen Eltern nach Amerika **fahren**,
or
Nächste Woche **werden wir** drei Tage in einem Hotel **wohnen**.

*Remember to put the infinitive (***fahren**, **wohnen**, *etc.) at the end of the phrase.*

You may already feel confident enough to talk about your last holidays, using the past (or perfect) tense. If not, don't worry, because there's a section later on in this chapter which will remind you how to do it.

German Revision Guide

Wortautomat

Wann machst du Urlaub / Ferien?
In den Sommerferien / Osterferien / Weihnachtsferien.

Mit wem fährst du in die Ferien?
Ich fahre mit meinem Vater / Bruder.
              meiner Mutter / Schwester.
              meinen Eltern / Freunden.

Wohin fahrt ihr?
Wir fahren…
    aufs Land.
    ans Meer.
    nach Berlin / Paris / London.
    nach Deutschland / Frankreich / Spanien / Italien / Österreich / Australien / Amerika.
    in die Schweiz.

Wie kommt ihr dahin?
Wir fahren mit dem Zug / Rad / Auto / Reisebus.
            mit der Fähre.
Wir fliegen (mit dem Flugzeug).

Wo übernachtet ihr?
    wohnt
Normalerweise   übernachten wir …
Meistens / Manchmal wohnen
Ab und zu
    in einer Jugendherberge / in Jugendherbergen.
    auf einem Campingplatz / auf Campingplätzen.
    in einem Hotel / in Hotels.
    bei Freunden / Verwandten.

Wie findest du das?
Ich finde das toll, denn…
    ich finde (viele) neue Freunde
    aus verschiedenen Ländern
    Deutsche / Österreicher / Schweizer / Franzosen / Engländer / Schotten / Irländer / Waliser / Spanier / Italiener / Amerikaner / Australier.

You will need a different set of words if you want to talk about languages or things instead of people. These are probably the most useful:
Deutsch / Französisch / Englisch / Walisisch / Spanisch / Italienisch.

When do you go on holiday?
In the summer / Easter / Christmas holidays.

Who do you go on holiday with?
I go with my dad / brother.
            my mum / sister.
            my parents / friends.

Where do you go?
We go…
    to the country.
    to the seaside.
    to Berlin / Paris / London.
    to Germany / France / Spain / Italy / Austria / Australia / America.
    to Switzerland.

How do you get there?
We go by train / bicycle / car / coach.
    by ferry.
We fly (by plane).

Where do you stay the night?
    stay?
Usually   we stay the night …
Mostly / Sometimes we stay …
From time to time
    in a youth hostel / in youth hostels.
    on a campsite / on campsites.
    in a hotel / in hotels.
    with friends / relations.

What do you think of it?
I think it's great, because…
    I make (lots) of new friends
    from different countries…
    Germans / Austrians / Swiss / French / English / Scottish / Irish / Welsh / Spaniards / Italians / Americans / Australians.

German / French / English / Welsh / Spanish / Italian.

billig / teuer
Es gibt (nur) ein Problem…
wenig für Vegetarier
wir essen (also) viele Käsebrote.

also in German means *so* in English! If you want to say *I also play tennis*, say **Ich spiele auch Tennis**. Watch out for word order too!

Das Essen im Hotel ist toll / schrecklich.
Das Hotel ist bequem / unbequem.

Pronunciation of **bequem** = 'bukvaym'

Es macht (keinen) Spaß!

Wie lange verbringt ihr im Urlaub?
Wir verbringen eine Woche   im Urlaub.
    zwei Wochen
    zehn Tage

Was für Ausflüge macht ihr?
Wir wandern (in den Bergen).
    schwimmen (im Meer).
    fahren Rad.
    spielen Tennis / Fußball.
    tanzen (in der Disco).
    besichtigen Burgen und Schlösser.
    kaufen Andenken / Souvenirs.

Wann fährst du zum nächsten Mal in die Ferien?
In einer Woche.
In zwei Wochen.
Diesen Sommer.
Im August.
In den Sommerferien.
Nächstes Jahr.
Nächsten Sommer / Juli.
In den nächsten Sommerferien.

Wohin fährst du am liebsten in den Ferien?
Ich fahre am liebsten nach Spanien, denn…
das Wetter ist schön heiß.
ich kann in der Sonne liegen,
   um braun zu werden.
Ich finde die Gegend sehr interessant / schön.
Es gibt viele interessante Sehenswürdigkeiten.
Es gibt dort viel zu tun / zu sehen.

Wie kommst du am liebsten dahin?
Wir fliegen   dahin.
Wir fahren mit dem Auto

cheap / expensive
There's (only) one problem …
not much for vegetarians
(So) we eat lots of cheese sandwiches.

The food in the hotel is great / terrible.
The hotel is comfortable / uncomfortable.

It's (no) fun!

How long do you spend on holiday?
We spend a week   on holiday.
    two weeks
    ten days

What sort of trips do you go on?
We go walking (in the hills).
    swim (in the sea).
    cycle / go on bike rides.
    play tennis / football.
    dance (at the disco).
    visit castles and stately homes.
    buy souvenirs.

When are you next going on holiday?
In a week.
In two weeks.
This summer.
In August.
In the summer holidays.
Next year.
Next summer / July.
Next summer holidays.

Where do you prefer to go for your holidays?
I prefer to go to Spain because…
the weather is nice and hot.
I can sunbathe
   to get a tan.
I find the area very interesting / beautiful.
There are lots of interesting sights.
There's lots to do / see there.

How do you prefer to travel there?
We fly there.
We go there by car.

Das ist viel schneller.
           bequemer.
           billiger.

It's much faster.
      more comfortable.
      cheaper.

Was machst du (gern) in den Ferien?
Morgens / Nachmittags / Abends
Ich stehe spät / früh auf.
Ich gehe direkt zum Strand(café),
wo ich Berliner mit Schokolade esse.

What do you (like to) do on holiday?
In the morning / afternoon / evening
I get up late / early.
I go straight to the beach (café),
where I eat doughnuts with chocolate.

Wo looks impressive if you want to say what you do in a particular place, but remember to put the verb at the end of the phrase.

Ich schwimme im Meer.
Ich liege in der Sonne.
Ich mache Siesta.
Dann bin ich (noch) zwei Stunden am Strand.

I swim in the sea.
I sun-bathe.
I have a siesta.
Then I spend (another) two hours on the beach.

Was macht dein Bruder / deine Schwester?
Was machen deine Eltern?

What does your brother / sister do?
What do your parents do?

Remember, you can use the same vocabulary to talk about what other people do, but don't forget to change the verbs!

Mein Bruder / Meine Schwester…
   steht auf / geht / **isst** / schwimm**t** /
   lieg**t** in der Sonne / mach**t** / ist…
Meine Eltern…
   steh**en** auf / geh**en** / ess**en** / schwimm**en** /
   lieg**en** in der Sonne / mach**en** / sind…
Meine Eltern sind schon seit eineinhalb
   Stunden am Strand.

My brother / sister…
   gets up / goes / eats / swims / sunbathes / does / is…
My parents…
   get up / go / eat / swim / sunbathe / do / are…

My parents have already been on the beach for one and a half hours.

Was kann man sonst machen?
Man kann einkaufen gehen.
           plaudern.
           die ganze Nacht tanzen.
Es gibt viele hübsche Jungs / Mädchen.

What else can you do?
You can go shopping.
   chat.
   dance all night.
There are lots of good-looking boys / girls.

Wann und wo esst ihr?
Gegen… Uhr gehen wir ins Restaurant / Café.
                         zur Imbissstube.
eine Menge Engländer
Wenn wir nach Hause fahren, bin ich immer
   traurig.

When and where do you eat?
At about… o'clock we go to the restaurant / café.
                         to the snack-bar.
lots of English people
When we go back home I'm always sad.

Base instinct

Frau Grün and Gretchen have been looking through some leaflets on camping and youth hostelling in the Black Forest and have decided to book this year's holiday without consulting Gerhard; if it's already sorted, he can't spoil things by saying he's going somewhere else with Marlene. Of course, he might want to invite her along, but there's no danger *she'd* be interested in three weeks of fresh air and hearty exercise.

It seems a good idea to split the holiday between a campsite and a youth hostel. This is the letter Frau Grün writes to the campsite:

```
Sehr geehrte Damen und Herren!

Wir fahren im Juli nach Nirgendbach. Wir
kommen am 12. Juli an, und möchten zehn
Nächte auf dem Campingplatz am Ende der
Welt bleiben. Bitte reservieren Sie Platz
für zwei Zelte. Wir sind eine Erwachsene
und zwei Kinder von 10 und 16 Jahren. Wir
habe kein Auto, aber wir bringen unsere
Fahrräder mit.

Mit freundlichen Grüßen,

Gertrud Grün.
```

Now that she's written the letter to the campsite, Frau Grün asks Gretchen to write to the Youth Hostel in Nirgendbach. She will need to reserve places for a woman, a girl and a boy for 11 nights from July 22nd. Gretchen is asking you to write the letter for her as she is too young to write important letters. Don't worry – you'll find all the words you need in the **Wortautomat**.

When you've written Gretchen's letter, imagine that you are planning a holiday with a group of friends. First of all, decide on the details (how many are going, where you'd like to stay, etc.), and then write your own letter, using as many of the **Wortautomat** expressions as you can.

Wortautomat

Sehr geehrte Damen und Herren!   Dear Sir / Madam,
Sehr geehrter Herr Schmidt!   Dear Mr Schmidt,
Lieber Herr Schmidt!
Sehr geehrte Frau Schäfer!   Dear Mrs Schäfer,
Liebe Frau Schäfer!

 *Use **Sehr geehrte(r)** if you don't know the person you're writing to, otherwise use **Liebe(r)**.*

Wir kommen am 12. Juli an.   We arrive on July 12th.
Wir fahren am 22. Juli ab.   We leave on July 22nd.
Wir möchten… Nächte auf dem Campingplatz bleiben.   We would like to stay… nights at the campsite.
                in der Jugendherberge   youth hostel.
                im Hotel   hotel.

*Saying **stay** in German: use **bleiben** if you're talking about how long you're staying somewhere; use **übernachten** or **wohnen** to explain where you're sleeping, e.g.*

Ich bleibe hier drei Tage.	I'm staying here for three days.
Ich übernachte / wohne im *Hotel am See*.	I'm staying in the *Hotel am See*.
Bitte reservieren Sie	Please reserve
Platz für ein Zelt / einen Wohnwagen.	a place for one tent / caravan.
Haben Sie zwei Zelte?	Have you got places for two tents?
drei Mädchen und zwei Jungen?	three girls and two boys?
ein / zwei Zimmer / Doppelzimmer mit Dusche / Bad?	one / two rooms / double rooms with shower / bath?
Wir sind eine Erwachsene / Frau.	We are an adult / woman.
ein Erwachsener / Mann.	an adult / man.
ein Kind von 10 Jahren.	a 10-year old child.
zwei Erwachsene.	two adults.
zwei Kinder.	two children.
Wir bringen einen Hund / zwei Hunde mit.	We are bringing a dog / two dogs.
ein Auto	a car.
Können Sie mir bitte Informationen über Preise / das Hotel schicken?	Please could you send me information about prices / the hotel.
Mit freundlichen Grüßen	Yours sincerely

Heavy weather

Meanwhile, the Müllers are trying to organise a holiday on the Costa del Sol, and Marlene is refusing to go unless Gerhard is invited. All her parents can do is hope that the pair will have split up by July.

By the end of June, however, both families are seriously worried. Gerhard has started listening to very loud rock music and Marlene has taken up cycling and eating cabbage. It's beginning to seem like a good idea to leave both of them behind in Kippenstadt.

Before they set off on their holiday, Frau Grün and Gretchen listen to the weather forecast so that they can plan the first few days' activities. Listen to the cassette and fill in the table below as fully as you can, using the **Wortautomat** to help you. If you're doing Foundation Level, you can leave out Sunday in Southern Germany.

	Wetter	Höchst-temperatur
Norddeutschland		
Samstag		
Sonntag		
Süddeutschland		
Samstag		
Sonntagvormittag		
Sonntagnachmittag		

Answer

	Wetter	Höchst-temperatur
Norddeutschland		
Samstag	schön, warm, sonnig	28°
Sonntag	schön, warm, sonnig	28°
Süddeutschland		
Samstag	kühl, windig, Regen	18°
Sonntagvormittag	bewölkt, niederschlagsfrei, wärmer	
Sonntagnachmittag	Sonne	25°

You will also need to be able to talk about the weather at different times of the year and say what you like doing when it's hot, cold, raining, etc. Look again at the **Wortautomat** and practise answering the following questions. (A couple of examples have been done for you. Make sure you keep the same word order in your own answers!)

a) Wie ist das Wetter bei dir im Sommer / Herbst / Winter / Frühling?
Im Sommer ist es normalerweise warm und sonnig, aber manchmal regnet es und ab und zu ist es ziemlich kühl.
Im Herbst…

b) Was machst du gern, wenn es heiß ist?
wenn es regnet?
wenn es schneit?
Wenn es heiß ist, liege ich in der Sonne und lese Zeitschriften. Manchmal gehe ich auch schwimmen.
Wenn es regnet,…

c) Wie war das Wetter gestern?
Gestern hat es… / war es…

Wortautomat

Nord / Süd / Ost / West	North / South / East / West
Wie ist das Wetter?	**What's the weather like?**
…bei dir	…where you live
…das kommende Wochenende	…the coming weekend
…im Sommer / Herbst / Winter / Frühling	…in summer / autumn / winter / spring
Es ist schön / warm / sonnig / heiß / kalt / windig / wolkig / kühl / nass / regnerisch / neblig / stürmisch.	It's fine / warm / sunny / hot / cold / windy / cloudy / cool / wet / rainy / foggy / stormy.
Es regnet.	It's raining / It rains.
Es schneit.	It's snowing / It snows.
Es friert.	It's freezing / It freezes.
Es donnert / blitzt.	There's thunder / lightning.
die Jahreszeit	the season
30 Grad (im Schatten)	30°C (in the shade)
Es gibt ein Gewitter / einen Sturm.	There is a storm.
Es gab (viel) Regen / Eis / Schnee / Sonnenschein.	There was (a lot of) rain / ice / snow / sunshine.
Wie wird das Wetter morgen sein?	**What will the weather be like tomorrow?**
Es wird heiter sein.	It'll be bright.
schwül	muggy.
trocken / niederschlagsfrei	dry.
(stark) bewölkt	(heavily) overcast.
Es wird regnen.	It'll rain.
Wie war das Wetter gestern?	**What was the weather like yesterday?**
Es war kalt.	It was cold.
Es hat geregnet / geschneit / gefroren.	It rained / snowed / was freezing.
Es hat gedonnert / geblitzt.	There was thunder / lightning.
Tageshöchsttemperaturen	day's highest temperature
Tagestiefsttemperaturen	day's lowest temperature
weiterhin	continuing

At your service

Frau Müller, who is a keen driver, has decided that they will be taking the car to Spain this year instead of flying. Martin is now in a very bad mood as he doesn't like long journeys and if Marlene's allowed to stay at home, he doesn't see why he should be forced to go.

The day before they are due to set off, Frau Müller and Martin take the car to the petrol station to fill up. It's self-service, but to cheer him up, Frau Müller lets Martin pretend to be the attendant. (He enjoys this.)

Frau Müller	Volltanken, bitte.
Martin	Super oder Bleifrei?
Frau Müller	Diesel, bitte.
Martin	Aber hier ist Selbstbedienung, gnädige Frau.
Frau Müller	Hier ist eine Mark.
Martin	In Ordnung. Sonst noch etwas?
Frau Müller	Bitte prüfen Sie den Reifendruck und das Öl und waschen Sie die Windschutzscheibe.
Martin	Noch eine Mark, bitte.

When you've made sure you understand the conversation, practise it with a friend until you know both parts by heart. (Use symbols to help you if you find the words hard to remember.)

When you are confident, have another look at the **Wortautomat**. You'll notice that it gives some extra phrases to do with car breakdown. With any luck, you won't need them in real life, but they may well be useful in your Speaking Test, so spend a few minutes memorising them.

Now imagine that you are driving with some friends through Germany and you're having problems with the car. You are the only German speaker in the group, so you call a local car mechanic for help. Tell him...

a) you're English, and you're on holiday here,
b) your car has broken down,
c) what sort of car you have,
d) the brakes don't work,
e) you also have a flat tyre.

Answers
a) Wir sind Engländer und sind hier auf Urlaub. b) Unser Auto hat eine Panne. c) Es ist ein BMW. d) Die Bremsen funktionieren nicht. e) Wir haben auch eine Reifenpanne.

Wortautomat

die Tankstelle	petrol station
die Werkstatt	garage
Volltanken, bitte.	Fill her up, please.
Super	4-star
Bleifrei	lead free
bleifreies Benzin	lead-free petrol
Diesel(benzin)	diesel
Für fünfzig Mark Super, bitte.	50 Marks worth of 4-star, please.
In Ordnung.	Fine.

Selbstbedienung	self-service
gnädige Frau	Madam
Bitte prüfen Sie den Reifendrück / das Öl.	Please would you check the tyre pressure / the oil.
die Windschutzscheibe	windscreen
die Bremsen	brakes
das Steuer	steering wheel
der Motor	engine
das Auto / der Wagen	car
der PKW (Personenkraftwagen)	car
der LKW (Lastkraftwagen)	lorry
das Motorrad	motorbike
das Mofa	moped
Unser Auto hat eine Panne.	Our car has broken down.
eine Reifenpanne	has a flat tyre.
Die Bremsen funktionieren nicht.	The brakes aren't working.
Das Auto ist ein Rolls Royce.	The car is a Rolls Royce.
Ich bin / Wir sind hier auf Urlaub.	I'm / We're on holiday here.

Hit and Miss

Meanwhile, in the Black Forest, Gretchen and Frau Grün have just returned to their campsite after a minor accident with a cat and a lamp-post. Frau Grün is now trying to bend her daughter's bike back into shape while Gretchen sits unhappily on her sleeping bag nursing a bruised arm and writing her first postcard to Gerhard.

Hallo! Ich habe gerade einen Radunfall gehabt! Mutti und ich fuhren durch ein kleines Dorf. Es war ganz regnerisch und die Straße war naß. Plötzlich habe ich etwas auf der Straße gesehen – es war eine kleine weiße Katze. Ich habe gebremst, doch die Straße war rutschig und ich bin gegen einen Laternenpfahl geschleudert. Die Katze war nicht verletzt, aber mein Fahrrad ist kaputt und ich habe einen großen blauen Fleck am Arm. Mutti ist jetzt böse, weil wir nicht mehr Rad fahren können, aber ich bin nicht schuld! Ich schreibe bald wieder! Dein Gretchen.

You are on holiday in Germany and have just witnessed an accident. Write a report of what you saw, using the pictures below to guide you.

Wortautomat

Ich habe (gerade) einen Unfall gehabt.	I've (just) had an accident.
Ich fuhr durch ein kleines Dorf / die Stadt.	I was driving / riding through a little village / the town.
Wir fuhren die Straße entlang.	We were along the road.
Ein rotes Auto fuhr zu schnell.	A red car was going too fast.
Ich ging in ein Geschäft.	I was going into a shop.
Ich war mit einer Freundin in einem Café.	I was with a friend in a café.
Es war regnerisch und die Straße war naß.	It was rainy and the road was wet.
Ein kleiner Junge überquerte die Straße.	A little boy was crossing the road.

 *These verbs are in the imperfect tense, which is used to say what was happening at a time in the past (I was walking, he was driving, etc). It's a good idea to learn a few of them in case you are asked to describe what was happening just before an accident. The most useful forms are **ich**, **er** / **sie** / **es** and **wir**. For more details, see page 139.)*

Plötzlich habe ich etwas auf der Straße gesehen.	Suddenly I saw something on the road.
Der Autofahrer hat den Jungen nicht gesehen.	The car driver didn't see the boy.
der Radfahrer	the cyclist
Ich habe / Er hat gebremst.	I / He braked.
rutschig / vereist	slippery / icy
Ich bin / Sie ist gegen einen Laternenpfahl geschleudert / gestoßen.	I / She skidded / bumped into a lamp-post.
Das Auto hat den Jungen überfahren.	The car ran the boy over.
Er ist gefallen.	He fell.
(schwer / leicht) verletzt	(badly / slightly) injured
tot	dead
kaputt	broken
Ich habe einen blauen Fleck am Arm / Bein.	I've got a bruise on my arm / leg.
Ich habe mir den Arm / das Bein gebrochen.	I broke my arm / leg.
Er / Sie hat sich	He / She his / her arm / leg.
Ich habe einen Krankenwagen gerufen.	I called an ambulance.
Der Krankenwagen hat mich / ihn / sie (sofort) ins Krankenhaus gefahren.	The ambulance took me / him / her (straight) to hospital.
böse	angry
Ich bin / war (nicht) schuld.	It is / was (not) my fault.

Ticket to ride

The next day, Frau Grün decides to take Gretchen to Baden-Baden, a beautiful spa town to the north of the Black Forest. As they cannot use their bikes until Gretchen's has been repaired, they jog to the nearest station, which is four miles up the road. Here's Frau Grün buying the tickets:

Frau Grün	Eineinhalbmal hin und zurück nach Baden-Baden.
Beamte	DM 32, bitte.
Frau Grün	Wann fährt der nächste Zug?
Beamte	Um zehn Uhr dreizehn.
Frau Grün	Und müssen wir umsteigen?
Beamte	Nein, der Zug fährt direkt.
Frau Grün	Von welchem Gleis fährt der Zug ab?
Beamte	Gleis 9.

You are at a station ticket office in Germany. Working with a friend or on your own, make up conversations using the following information:

Reiseziel	Fahrkarte	Preis	der nächste Zug	umsteigen?	Gleis
Stuttgart	1 x einfach	DM 12	18.51	direkt	6
Berlin	1½ x hin und zurück	DM 95.50	09.23	in Frankfurt	3
München	2 x hin und zurück	DM 46	14.15	direkt	1

Wortautomat

einfach	single ticket(s)
hin und zurück nach...	return ticket(s) to...
erste / zweite Klasse	first / second class
Wann fährt der nächste Zug (nach)...?	**When does the next train go (to)...?**
Wann kommt der Zug an?	**When does the train arrive?**
Gibt es einen Zug gegen zwei Uhr?	**Is there a train at around two o'clock?**
Müssen wir umsteigen?	**Do we have to change?**
Der Zug fährt direkt.	The train goes direct.
Von welchem Gleis fährt der Zug ab?	**Which platform does the train leave from?**
der Zuschlag	supplement
der Bahnhof	(railway) station
die Bushaltestelle	bus stop
der Flughafen	airport

German Revision Guide

Home alone

Back in Kippenstadt, Gerhard and Marlene are eating lots of salad and having wild parties every night. But they can't help missing their families just a little bit, and spend the first three mornings wondering why they haven't had any postcards yet. On the fourth morning Gretchen's first card arrives, and Gerhard worries that she may be more seriously hurt than anyone realises.

Over the next few days a whole batch of reassuring cards comes from both the Grüns and the Müllers, and he begins to feel OK again.

Here are a couple of the postcards. As it was raining in Kippenstadt when they were delivered, the names of the senders got smudged. Who do you think wrote them?

A) Hallo Marlene! Wie geht's? Mir geht's sehr gut! Das Wetter ist heiß und sonnig. Ich war heute morgen drei Stunden am Strand. Ich habe Handball gespielt und bin im Meer geschwommen. Es hat viel Spaß gemacht! Erinnerst Du Dich an Stefan? Er ist wieder da, aber mit einer neuen Freundin! Hoffentlich langweilst du dich nicht!

B) Hallo Gerhard! Hoffentlich geht's Dir gut. Gretchen und ich sind heute mit dem Zug nach Baden-Baden gefahren. So eine schöne Stadt! Wir sind im Kurpark spazieren gegangen und dann haben wir Kräutertee in einem kleinen Café getrunken. Schließlich haben wir eine Stadtrundfahrt gemacht. Sehr interessant! Bis bald! (Vergiss nicht, Geige zu üben!) Deine

Using the two postcards and the **Wortautomat**, it should be easy to write about your most recent holiday (real or imaginary). Give as many details as you can.

Answers: A Martin; B Frau Grün

Wortautomat

Ich war heute morgen drei Stunden am Strand.	I was on the beach this morning for three hours.
Es gab ein Problem.	There was a problem.
Ich hatte	I had
Es hat viel Spaß gemacht.	It was great fun.
Erinnerst du dich an…?	Do you remember…?
Vergiss nicht, Geige zu üben.	Don't forget to practise the violin.
Meine Freundin Helen ist mitgekommen.	My friend Helen came along.
Ich habe Handball gespielt.	I played handball.
Wir haben viel gemacht.	We did lots of things.
Kräutertee in einem kleinen Café getrunken.	drank herb tea in a small café.
eine Stadtrundfahrt gemacht.	did a tour around the town.
drei Nächte dort übernachtet.	stayed three nights there.
es toll gefunden.	found it fun.
jeden Tag Eis gegessen.	ate ice-cream every day.
zwei Wochen dort verbracht.	spent two weeks there.
die ganze Nacht getanzt.	danced all night.

Los geht's

	eine Burg besichtigt.	visited a castle.
	Andenken gekauft.	bought souvenirs.
	mit meinen Freunden geplaudert.	chatted with my friends.
Ich bin	im Meer geschwommen.	I swam in the sea.
Wir sind	mit dem Zug nach Baden-Baden gefahren.	We went to Baden-Baden by train.
	spazieren gegangen.	went for walks.
	nach München gefahren.	drove to Munich.
	nach Amerika geflogen.	flew to America.
	in den Bergen gewandert.	went rambling in the mountains.
	in der Sonne gelegen.	lay in the sun.
	jeden Tag spät aufgestanden.	got up late every day.
	in der Stadt einkaufen gegangen.	went shopping in town.

Letztes Jahr	Last year
In den letzten Sommerferien	In the last summer holidays
Letzten Juli	Last July
Vor zwei Jahren	Two years ago
Dann	Then
Danach	After that
Schließlich	Finally

*When you use phrases such as **letztes Jahr**, remember to change the word order so that the verb is the second idea e.g.:* Letztes Jahr **bin ich** nach Frankreich gefahren.

Well, it's time to leave the Grüns and the Müllers to get on with their own lives. We can only guess what will happen to Gerhard and Marlene in the end. Can Marlene really keep up the cycling? Will Gerhard still be listening to Bon Jovi this time next year? Can love conquer all?

At least you can be sure of one thing. If you've followed the exercises in this book, you'll get a better grade at GCSE!

Test Yourself

Task 1

You are on holiday in Germany and want to travel to Berlin by train. At the station you need to find out what time the next train goes, when it arrives, and whether you have to change trains. You also need to buy one second class return ticket.

What do you say?

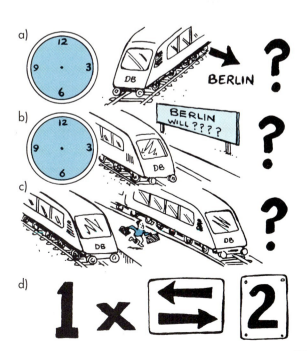

Task 2

Give a 1 – 2 minute talk on your holidays, using the Mind Map below to help you. Make sure you use the verbs in the right tenses (past, present or future) and use *time markers* to say what time period you are talking about.

Add *preferences* and *what other people do* to the Mind Map. Remember to give reasons for your opinions.

Task 3

Lies diese Wettervorhersage aus einer deutschen Zeitung:

Stark bewölkt und Regen, 16 bis 19 Grad

Fast den ganzen Tag über bleibt es stark bewölkt. Nur im Norden kommt örtlich die Sonne durch. In der Mitte und im Süden fällt häufig Regen, am Nachmittag gibt es Gewitter.

Richtig oder falsch?	Richtig	Falsch
a) Im Norden wird es sehr sonnig sein.	☐	☐
b) Die Tageshöchsttemperaturen werden weniger als 20 Grad sein.	☐	☐
c) Im Süden wird es donnern und blitzen.	☐	☐
d) In der Mitte wird es nass sein.	☐	☐

Answers

Task 1
a) Um wie viel Uhr fährt der nächste Zug nach Berlin?
b) Wann kommt der Zug an?
c) Muss ich umsteigen?
d) Einmal hin und zurück, zweite Klasse, bitte.

Task 3
a) Falsch; b) Richtig; c) Richtig; d) Richtig.

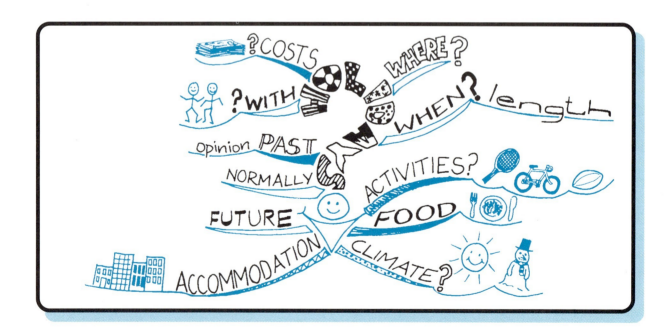

9 Putting it all together

Making sense of the instructions and rubrics

After all that hard work, you need to make sure that you understand the questions that the examiners are asking, otherwise you won't be able to impress them will all that hard-earned knowledge. Although individual questions vary, there are some instructions which are repeatedly used. The most common is:

- **Schreib** or **schreibe** (= write)

e.g. ...deinem / deiner Brieffreund / Brieffreundin einen Brief / eine Postkarte
(= Write a letter / postcard to your penfriend).

Schreibe
...ein paar Sätze (= Write a few sentences)

   ein Paar (= a pair), **ein paar** (= a few)

...nur ein paar Wörter (= just a few words)
...die richtigen Buchstaben / Nummer... neben das Bild / auf den Plan (= the correct letters / numbers... beside the picture / on the diagram)
...ja oder nein (= yes or no)
...die Zahl der Bilder neben den richtigen Abschnitt (= the number of the pictures against the correct extract)
...mit folgenden Informationen (= ...with the following information)
...ungefähr 120 Wörter (= about 120 words)

Other ways of telling you to write something include:
- **Beschreibe...** (= Describe...)
- **Beantworte die Frage auf Deutsch.** (= Answer the question in German.)
- **Kreuze A, B oder C an.** (= Put a cross at A, B or C.)
- **Kreuze nur einen Satz / ein Bild an.** (= Put a cross by only one sentence / picture.)
- **Kreuze die Bilder an, die zur Geschichte gehören.** (= Mark with a cross the pictures which belong to / go with the story.)
- **Wähle die richtigen Antworten.** (= Choose the right answers.)
- **Fülle diesen Studenplan auf Deutsch aus.** (= Complete / fill in this timetable in German.)
- **Vervollständige die Sätze.** (= Complete the sentences.)
- **Was ist richtig / falsch / nicht im Lesetext.** (= What is true / false / not in the text?)

Sometimes the examiner will suggest ideas for an answer. E.g.

- **Du könntest die folgenden Fragen beantworten.** (= You could answer the following questions.)
- **Lies die Texte.** (= Read the texts / passages.)
- **Sieh die Bilder an.** (= Look at the pictures.)
- **Hör den Text an.** (= Listen to the passage.)
- **Hör gut zu, dann beantworte die folgenden Fragen.** (= Listen carefully, then answer the following questions.)

These are the most common instructions. You may occasionally be given a task which is worded slightly differently, but what you have to do will be obvious from the context, and in any case will almost certainly use the vocabulary given above.

Areas of experience

Unless you are taking a modular course in German, your syllabus will be divided into five areas of experience:
A) Everyday activities
B) Personal and social life
C) The world around us
D) The world of work
E) The international world

Most students will need to know about all five areas. If you are taking the shortened course, you will probably not be examined on all of them, but always check with your teacher before leaving anything out. This section summarises the five areas in Mind Map form. Everyone needs the Foundation Level material on the Mind Maps, but only those taking the Higher Level need the extra material in the boxes.

 When you are revising, see how many different uses you can find for the same information. E.g. information about accommodation might be useful when describing your home, your holiday or even work experience and could feature in all five areas of experience.

German Revision Guide

A Everyday activities

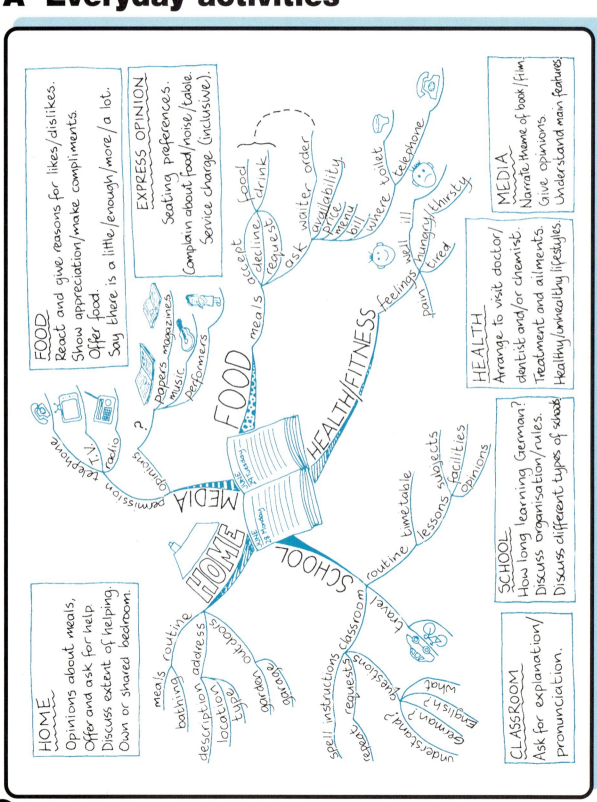

B Personal and social life

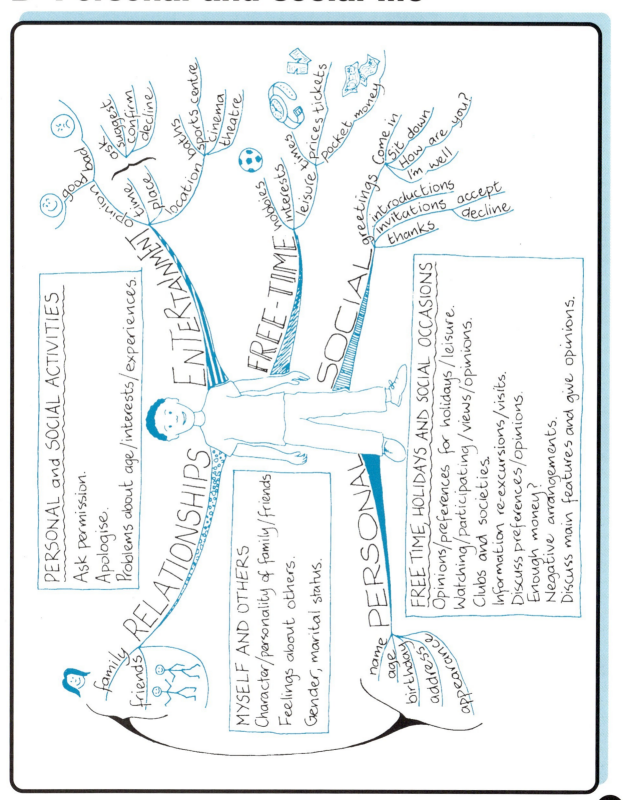

C The world around us

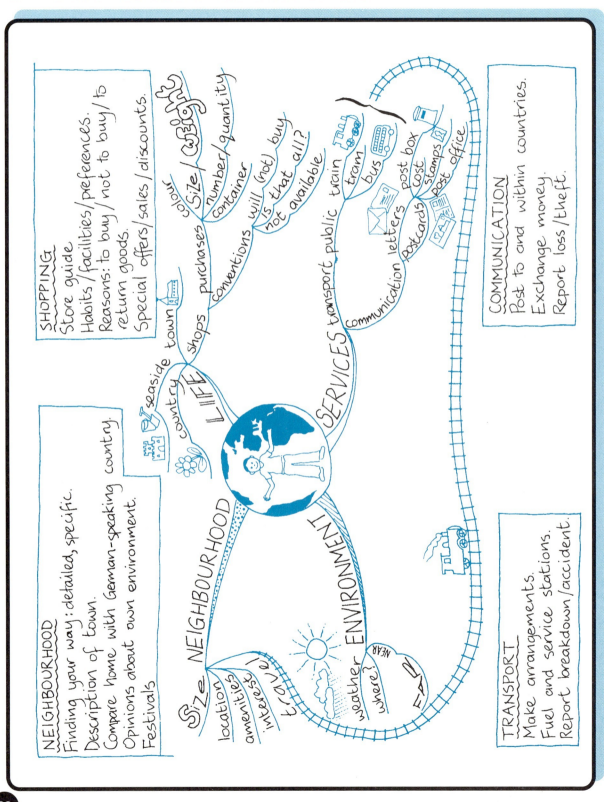

D The world of work

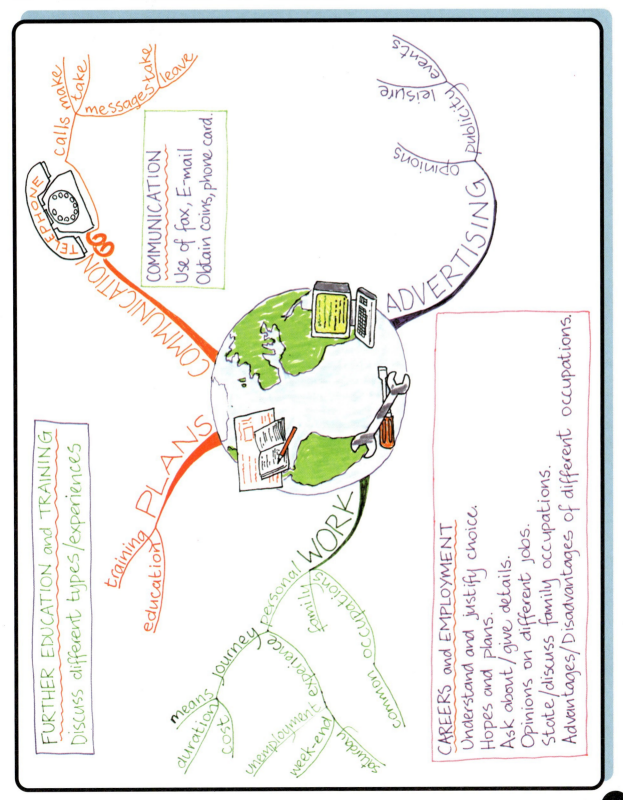

E The international world

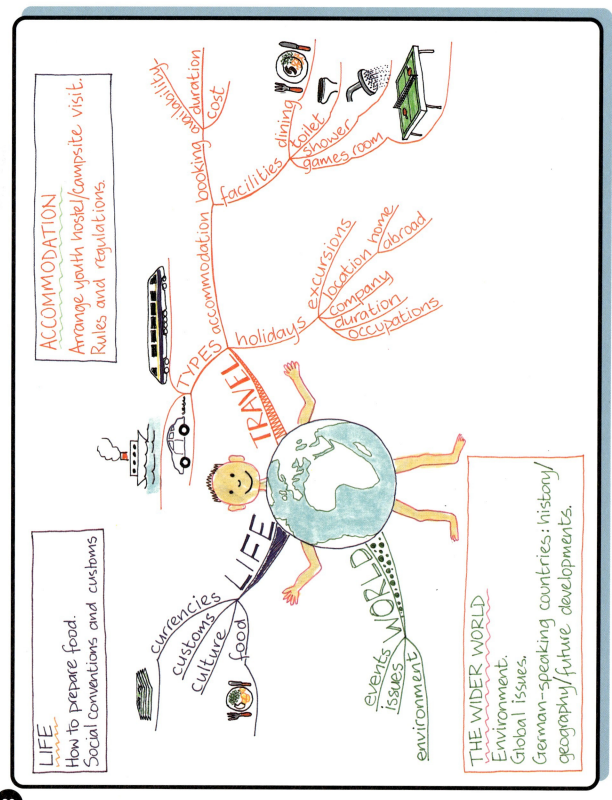

10 Meet the Memory Joggers

This chapter is designed to help you consolidate what you have learned, to show you any weak points you might have and to suggest ways in which you can use Mind Maps and pictures to create your own personal German fitness programme.

Try putting yourself in the examiner's place: in preparing the questions he or she asks him/herself: *Does this candidate know…?, Can the candidate describe…?*, and so on. Our Memory Joggers get in first, by making sure that you don't get caught out on the exam day.

Here are the individual subjects:

TIME
SEASONS
DATES
NUMBERS
WEATHER
YOUR HOME
COLOURS
RELATIONS
HELPING OUT
SPORT AND LEISURE
FOOD
SHOPPING
CLOTHES
ILLNESS
PARTS OF THE BODY
DIRECTIONS
RAILWAY STATION
COUNTRIES
LANGUAGES
SCHOOL
HOLIDAYS
QUESTIONS
ALPHABET
FAHREN
DER HOF
HAUPT-

Everybody's ideas and mental pictures are different. If you can improve on the pictures and Mind Maps on the following pages, then draw out your own version. Remember that the best Memory Joggers are the ones that work for you.

Now start training with these Memory Joggers:

10 time is it?

Martin Müller hates school so much that he constantly watches the clock to work out how much time is left to be endured in every lesson. Most lessons begin on the hour and last 60 minutes.

At first, Martin happily counts the minutes which have passed.

A quarter of the way through the lesson Martin is disappointed that only 15 minutes have gone by – it seems much longer to him in most lessons and especially those that he really hates.

Martin's spirits can drop even further after 30 minutes because there are still 30 minutes to go before the end of the lesson.

After another five minutes Martin realises that he is on the home straight.

Following many complaints from teachers about Martin's clock-watching habits, his mother buys him a digital watch with the 24-hour clock in the hope that this will cure Martin's clock watching. But it doesn't! He still spends the lessons counting the minutes to go until he can escape the classroom.

 Use the 24-hour clock in German as you do in English. This is often useful in travel situations or for TV programmes. Take care not to mix the two systems: 12- and 24-hour.

Half past comes up frequently in exam listening comprehension exercises. In a situation where time is involved, write down the word **halb** as soon as you hear it; remember Martin's experience of being half way to the next hour.

time of year is it?

Remember: each season is **der**, but it's **die Jahreszeit**.

Früh (= early) → **der Frühling** (= springtime)
das Jahr (= year)
die Zeit (= time) → **die Jahreszeit** (= season)

10

many?

Leave out the 'one' in numbers such as 105: **hundertfünf** or 1008: **tausendacht**.

did you come?

5th	**fünfte**	11th	**elfte**
6th	**sechste**	12th	**zwölfte**
7th	**siebte**	13th	**dreizehnte**
8th	**achte**	20th	**zwanzigste**
9th	**neunte**	30th	**dreißigste**
10th	**zehnte**		

Meet the Memory Joggers

is the weather like?

*By adding **nicht** you can double the number of things you can say! For example, if the weather is bad, you can say: **Die Sonne scheint nicht**; if the weather is dry, you can say: **Es regnet nicht**. There is no capital letter form of ß. **heiß** = **HEISS**.*

10 do you live?

is it like?

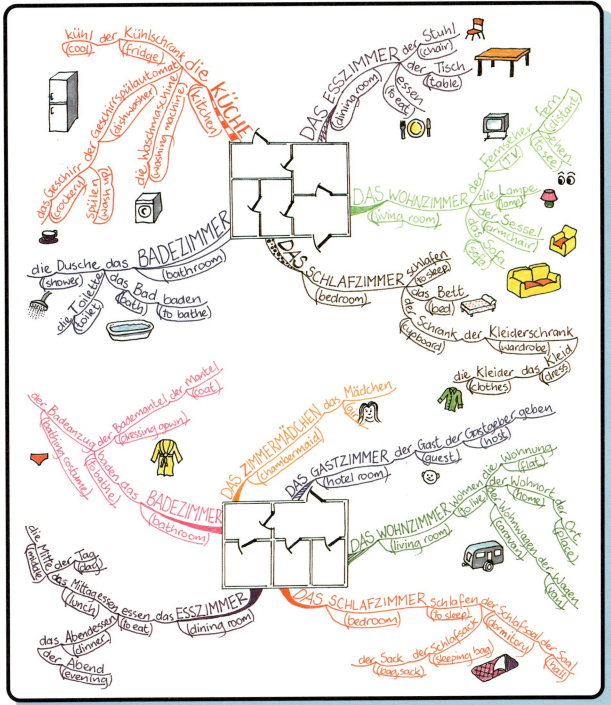

die Treppe (= stairs)
die Tür (= door)

das Eßzimmer (or ESSZIMMER)

10

 colour is it?

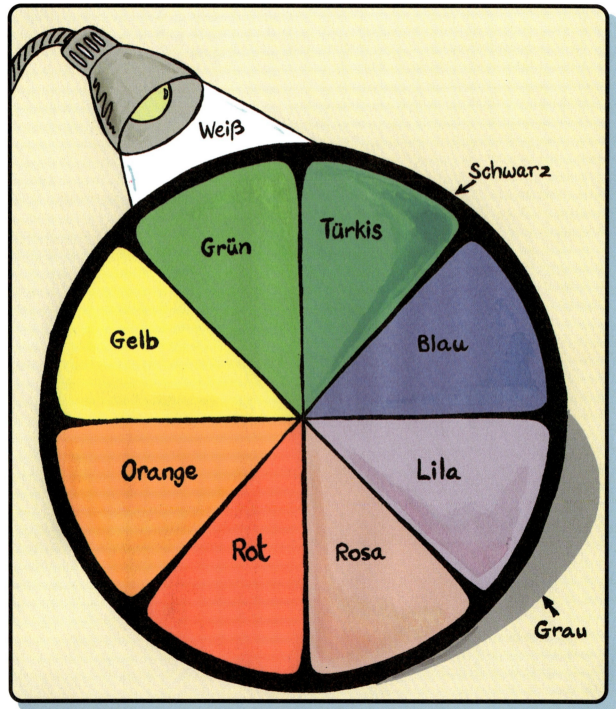

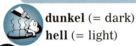 **dunkel** (= dark)
hell (= light)

braun (= brown)
blond (= blonde)

Meet the Memory Joggers

's in your family?

 der Junge (= boy)   **das Mädchen** (= girl)   **die Zwillinge** (= twins)

10 do you help at home?

Meet the Memory Joggers

 do you do in your spare time?

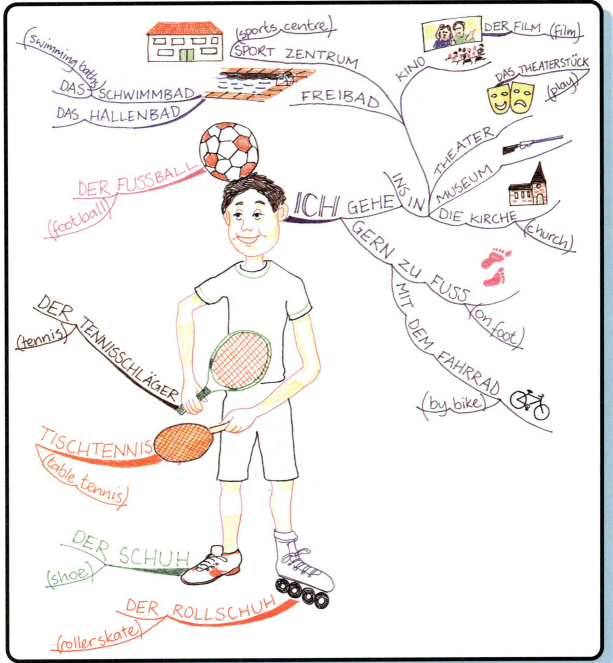

 Remember: if you don't like doing something, just insert a **nicht** *in front of* **gern**. *E.g.* **Ich gehe nicht gern ins Kino.**

10 would you like?

 das Getränk (= drink)   (**die Getränke** = drinks)
der Kuchen (= cake)   (**die Kuchen** = cakes)
die Küche (= kitchen)   (**die Küchen** = kitchens)
das Menü (= fixed price menu)

zahlen (= to pay)
Zahlen bitte! / Die Rechnung bitte!
(= Could I have the bill, please?)

fruit and vegetables are there?

 Most useful vegetables:

die Kartoffel (= potato)   (**die Kartoffeln** = potatoes)   **der Kohl** (= cabbage)
die Tomate (= tomato)   (**die Tomaten** = tomatoes)   **die Zwiebel** (= onion)

German Revision Guide

10

 are you buying?

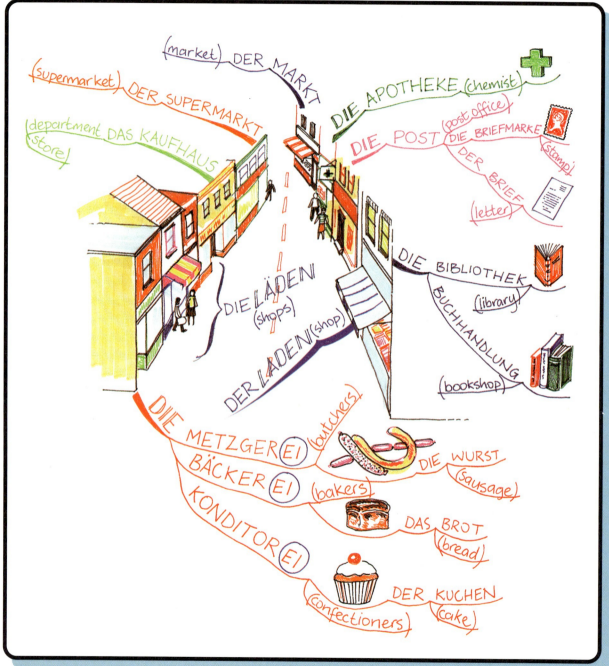

Have you noticed that most shops are feminine?

are you wearing?

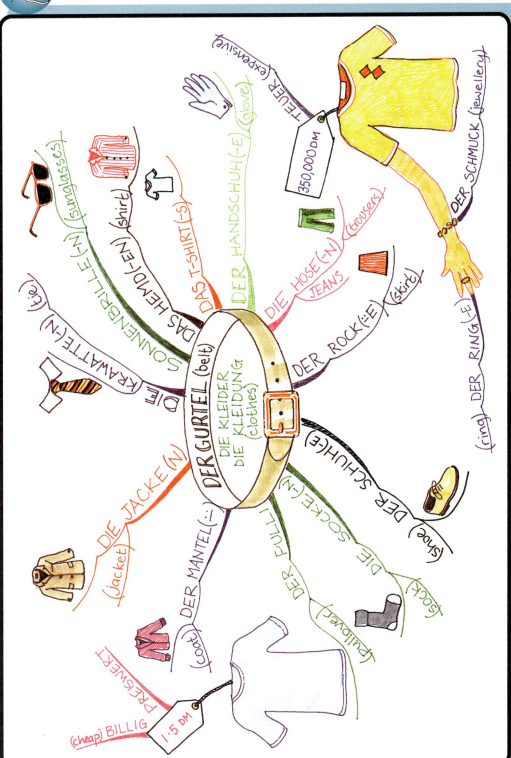

- der **Stoff** (= material)
- das **Leder** (= leather)
- die **Wolle** (= Wolle)
- die **Baumwolle** (= cotton)
- der **Baum** (= tree)

(die **Stoffe** = materials)

- die **Kleider** (= clothes)
- das **Kleid** (= dress)

10 's wrong?

Meet the Memory Joggers

 does it hurt?

German Revision Guide

 way?

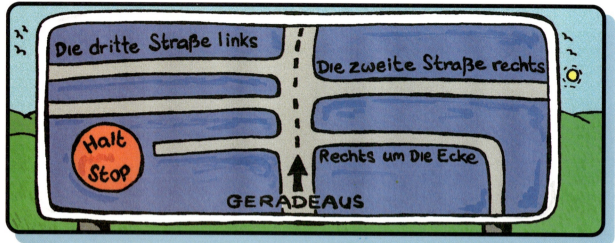

 is...?

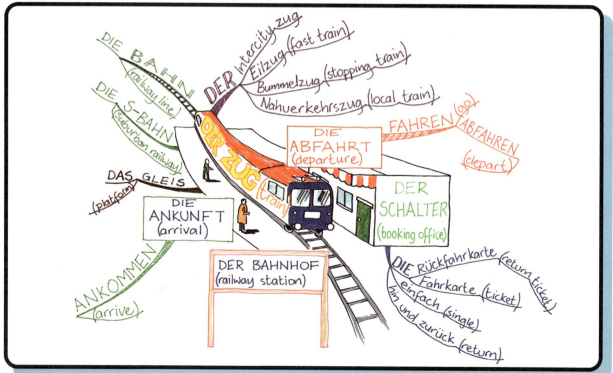

 Abfahren and **ankommen** are separable verbs.
Wann **fährt** der nächste Zug **ab**? (= When does the next train leave?)
Wann **kommt** der nächste Zug **an**? (= When does the next train arrive?)

Meet the Memory Joggers

 are you from?

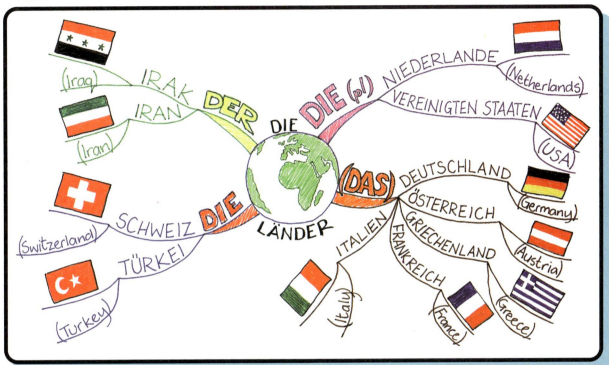

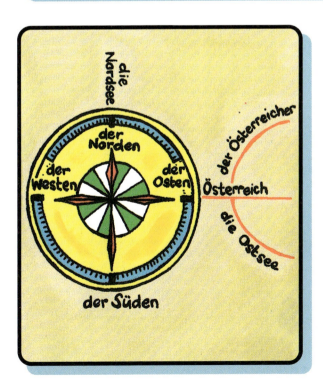

10 What do you speak?

Remember: Ich spreche Englisch; Ich bin Engländer / Engländerin.

Meet the Memory Joggers

 do you learn?

Remember: **lernen** (= to learn), + **lehren** (to teach)

is your school like?

Remember: **die Turnhalle** (= gymnasium)
das Gymnasium (= grammar school)
die Gesamtschule (= comprehensive school)

do you do on holiday?

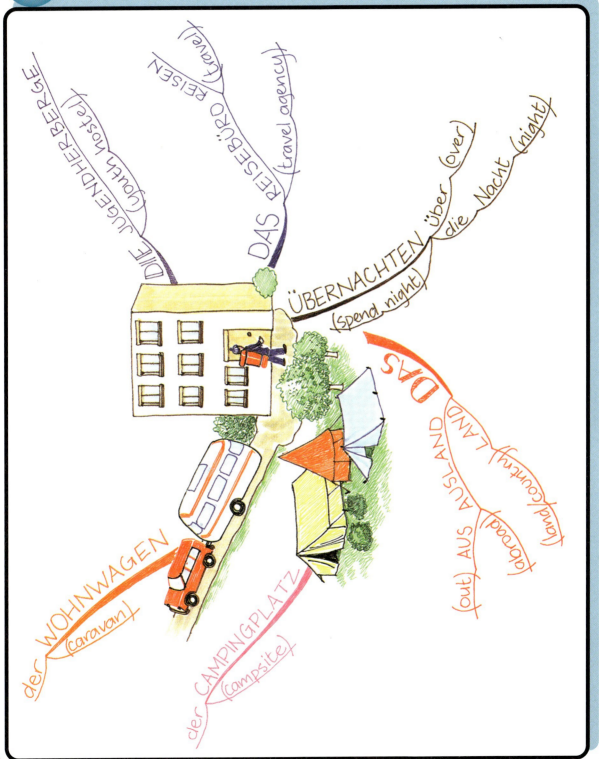

question words are there?

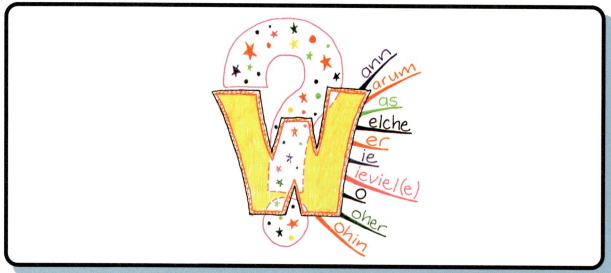

Question words are always followed immediately by a verb.

Was machst du? (= What are you doing?)
Wie heißt es? (= What is it called?)
Wo ist er? (= Where is he?)

Wann kommt sie? (= When is she coming?)

If you answer a question about yourself, e.g. **Wo wohnst du?** (= Where do you live?) *remember to change the verb form*: **Ich wohne in einer kleinen Stadt.** (= I live in a small town.)

 does the alphabet sound?

'Do it yourself'

These pictures and Mind Maps should have given your memory a hefty jog! Now think about your personal circumstances and how you would talk about them in German:

- What do you look like?
- Who are your friends?
- What do you like doing?
- What don't you like?
- How do you spend your day?
- Who is in your family?
- What do you want to do when you leave school?

These are the kind of thing you might be asked. If you've thought of the answers beforehand, and can speak them confidently, you will appear to be amazingly fluent! Try drawing your own Memory Joggers and prepare to astonish those examiners!

Some German words have lots of relations; this fact can save you time and effort when learning vocabulary. See **fahren**, **der Hof** and **Haupt-** below and on page 124.

Other joggers are **halten** (= to hold, keep), **geben** (= to give), and **fern** (= distant) – think of **fernsehen** and **fernsprechen**; then develop **sehen** and **sprechen**. Once you start thinking like this, you will remember an amazing amount of vocabulary without really trying. Collect words that have the same structure; try nouns with the same plural form, or strong / irregular verbs.

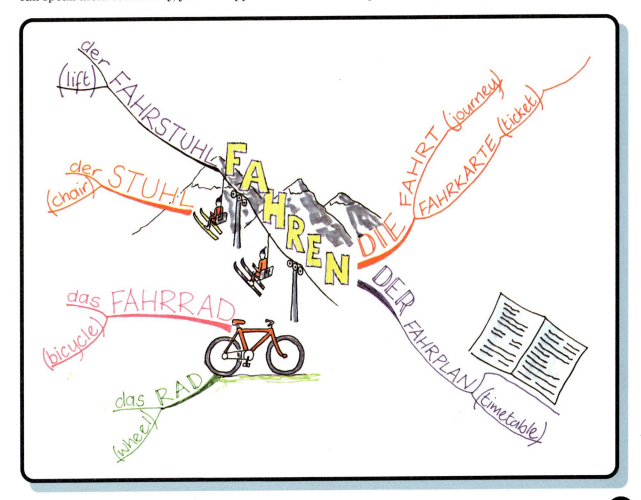

10

German Revision Guide

11 Grammar

Frau Grün gets to grips with grammar

Do you groan at the mere mention of German grammar? Don't despair. Help is at hand in the unlikely form of Frau Grün's store cupboard. In it you'll find most of the German grammar you will need for success at GCSE as well as explanations that you'll find easy to remember.

Here's what's in the cupboard:

1 **Nouns**
    The gender question
        Masculine nouns
        Feminine nouns
        Neuter nouns
        Plurals
 Using a dictionary
        Pronouns
        Personal pronouns
        Interrogative pronouns

2 **Cases**
    The nominative case
    The accusative case
    The genitive case
    The dative case

3 **Adjectives**
    The agreeable Grüns
    Demonstrative adjectives
    Using **ein** or **kein**
 A sneaky tip

4 **Adverbs**

5 **Adjectives: comparative / superlative**

6 **Adverbs: comparative / superlative**

7 **Prepositions**
    …always followed by the accusative
    …always followed by the dative case
    …followed by either the accusative or the dative case
    …always followed by the genitive case
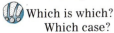 Which is which?
    Which case?

8 **Verbs**
    Energy-saving infinitives
    The future with infinitives
    Frau Grün's alternative
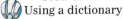 Using a dictionary
    Mystery modals
    Martin's modal magnets
    Feeling weak or strong?
    Reflexive verbs
    Imperatives and reflexives
    Impersonal verbs
    Passive verbs

9 **Tenses**
    Present
    Imperfect
    Separable verbs
        …present and imperfect
        …future
        …perfect
    Perfect
    Frau Grün's perfect sarnies
    Haben or **sein**?
 Another sneaky tip
    Past participles
    Inseparable verbs

10 **Word order**
    More of Martin's magnets
    Getting everything in order
    Asking questions
    Wann? Wo? Wie?
    Three more magnets

11 **Conjunctions**

1 Nouns

The gender question – By now you probably know that nouns, (i.e. the names of people, places, or things) in German are either masculine, feminine or neuter. This can be a great nuisance as far as non-native German speakers are concerned, but the tidy-minded Frau Grün has done her best to make the task a little easier: she has set up separate gender bins with labels on the bins to help her remember which one to use.

Masculine nouns

Into the bin for *masculine* nouns, Frau Grün puts many of the following:
- male persons, e.g.

der König	king
der Arzt	doctor

- seasons, months and days of the week, e.g.

der Winter	winter
der Januar	January
der Montag	Monday

- wind and weather, e.g.

der Wind	wind
der Schnee	snow
der Regen	rain

- nouns ending in **-ast** or **-ig**, e.g.

der Gast	guest
der Honig	honey

Feminine nouns

Frau Grün puts these nouns into the *feminine* bin:
- nouns which refer to females (but not those ending in **-chen** or **-lein**), e.g.

die Frau	wife, woman
die Königin	queen

- nouns which end in **-ei**, **-ie**, **-heit**, **-keit**, **-schaft** and **-ung**, e.g.

die Bäckerei	bakery
die Industrie	industry
die Gesundheit	health
die Möglichkeit	possibility
die Landschaft	scenery
die Wohnung	flat

Neuter Nouns

Frau Grün has one important set of nouns in the *neuter* bin:
- young persons and animals; these end in **-chen** and **-lein**, e.g.

das Mädchen	girl
das Fräulein	young woman

Included in her mixed assortment of other nouns are letters of the alphabet.
das Alphabet
das 'E'

 der See = lake, but **die** See = sea.

This is easier to sort out if you remember that **die** rhymes with 'sea'.

Try as she might, Frau Grün can't stuff everything she wants into her preferred bin: you will find that there are some nouns which do not fit into the rules, so it really does save time and effort in the long run to learn each new noun with its gender and plural.

You might find it helpful to imagine or draw pictures in which all the items are of the same gender.

Grammar

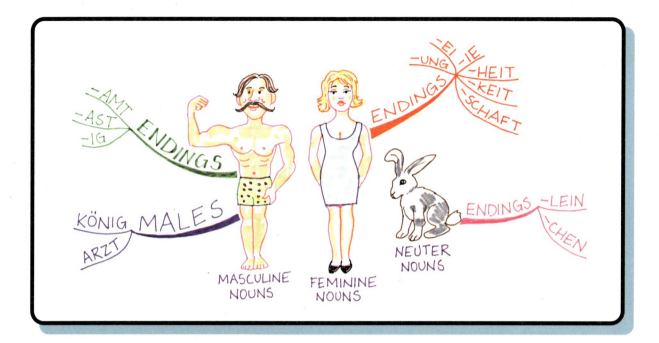

Plurals

🙁 Let's get the bad news over first!
There are no absolute rules which govern the way in which a German noun makes its plural, and to be completely safe, you need to learn each one as you progress.

🙂 Now for the good news!
There are a few patterns which come up over and over again, and many of the nouns which you need for your exam belong to one of these groups.

- Most masculine nouns ending in **-el**, **-en**, or **-er** don't change in the plural, although some add an umlaut to a previous **a**, **o** or **u**, e.g.
  der Onkel → die Onkel
  der Bäcker → die Bäcker
  der Vater → die Väter
  der Bruder → die Brüder

- Most of the other masculine nouns that you will meet take **-e** or **-̈e**, e.g.
  der Schuh → die Schuhe
  der Hund → die Hunde
  der Arm → die Arme
  der Tag → die Tage
  der Fuß → die Füße
  der Stuhl → die Stühle

- Nearly all feminine nouns add **-en** or **-n** in the plural, e.g.
  die Frau → die Frauen
  die Wohnung → die Wohnungen
  die Bäckerei → die Bäckereien
  die Industrie → die Industrien

- There is no change to any of the neuter nouns ending in **-chen** or **-lein**, nor to most of those ending in **-el**, **-en**, **-er**, e.g.
  das Mädchen → die Mädchen
  das Segel → die Segel
  das Messer → die Messer
  das Kissen → die Kissen
  das Kopfkissen → die Kopfkissen

- Monosyllabic neuter nouns (i.e. those with one syllable) often add **-er**, or **-̈er**, e.g.
  das Blatt → die Blätter
  das Haus → die Häuser
  das Dorf → die Dörfer
  das Tal → die Täler
  das Kind → die Kinder

- Most of the other neuter nouns add **-e**, e.g.
  das Spiel → die Spiele
  das Tier → die Tiere
  das Jahr → die Jahre
  das Bein → die Beine

As with German genders, you will find other common patterns that occur with the plural forms. Although at times you will probably find that you do need to learn vocabulary, it gets much easier if you start to use, and keep on using, new words and expressions as you come across them.

Using a dictionary

If your exam includes course work which you prepare in advance, it makes sense to check the gender and plural of any noun of which you are unsure. You can also use a dictionary in some of the examinations, so to save time on the day, familiarise yourself in advance with the way your dictionary works.

Some dictionaries have *English – German* followed by *German – English*, while others are the reverse. Knowing in advance which way round your dictionary works saves valuable minutes because you can immediately open the book in the right area.

English – German: the dictionary will give you the German translation of the English word that you look up, followed by its gender – either in the abbreviated form (m), (f), or (n), or as **der**, **die**, or **das**.

> **dog** n. Hund *der*
> **dog** ~**biscuit** n. Hundekuchen *der*
> ~**collar** (Hunde)halsband *das*
> a ~**eared book** ein Buch mit Eselsohren

German – English: if you need to look up a plural form, you will need this part of the dictionary. After the gender, you will probably find either the plural form written out, or two endings in brackets, e.g. (-s; -) or (-; -n). The **second abbreviation** gives the plural, so in the first example, (-s; -), the plural form is the same as the singular, while in the second example, (-; -n), the plural form would add an **-n**.

Singular		Plural
der Kuchen	cake	Kuchen
die Freundschaft	friendship	Freundschaften
das Blatt	leaf	Blätter

Pronouns

These are words which take the place of nouns. For example, instead of saying, *The dog bit the postman* you can say, *He bit **him***, provided that everybody first understands who the *he* and *him* are. By this stage, you might find that you are using many of these pronouns in German without consciously thinking about them, but they are given here for reference – and to make you feel good if you can already use them! See below for explanation of the cases.

Interrogative pronouns

When Frau Grün demands to know, *Who's coming today?*, *Who(m) will you see later?* or *To whom are you giving the book?*, she needs to use the interrogative pronouns, i.e.
Wer? (= who), **Wen?** (= whom) and **Wem?** (= to whom). E.g.

Wer kommt heute?	Who's coming today?
Wen sehen Sie später?	Who(m) will you see later?
Wem gibst du dieses Buch?	To whom are you giving this book?

 Remember: **Wer?** (= who) and **Wo?** / **Wohin?** (= where). See page 144.

Personal pronouns

nominative case		accusative		dative	
I	ich	me	mich	to me	mir
you (singular, familiar form)	du	you	dich	to you	dir
you (singular, polite form)	Sie	you	Sie	to you	Ihnen
he / she / it	er / sie / es	him / her / it	ihn / sie / es	to him / to her / to it	ihm / ihr / ihm
we	wir	us	uns	to us	uns
you (plural, familiar form)	ihr	you	euch	to you	euch
you (plural, polite form)	Sie	you	Sie	to you	Ihnen
they	sie	them	sie	to them	ihnen

2 Cases

Frau Grün keeps suitcases in her store cupboard! – As you have no doubt noticed, German has more than one way of saying *the* or *a*. The various forms are called 'cases', and Frau Grün has four. She is very particular about choosing the right outfit from the right case for every occasion.

The nominative case

When does Frau Grün use the nominative case? She uses it when the noun (naming word) is the subject (person doing) of the verb (doing word), e.g.

Der Junge läuft.	The boy is running / the boy runs.

is running or *runs* tell you what the person is 'doing', and the subject, or person doing the running, is the boy. As well as doing, verbs can describe 'being' or 'becoming', e.g.

Der Hund ist alt.	The dog is old.
Das Kaninchen ist hungrig.	The rabbit is hungry.
Die Leute sind böse.	The people are angry.
Die Frau wird müde	The woman is becoming / getting tired.

The verb in each of these sentences is either **ist** (= is), **sind** (= are), or **wird** (= is getting / becoming).

The accusative case

When does Frau Grün use the accusative case? She uses it when the *noun* is the object of the verb, i.e. is having something done to it, e.g.

Der Mann hält **den** Stock.	The man holds the stick.
Das Kaninchen sieht **die** Torte.	The rabbit sees the flan.
Die Frau singt **das** Lied.	The woman sings the song.
Das Mädchen trägt **die** Bücher.	The girl carries the books.

Or after certain prepositions, e.g.

Frau Grün geht in **den** Garten.	Frau Grün goes into the garden.
Durch **das** ganze Jahr.	Throughout the whole year.

You will find out more about prepositions on page 133.

The genitive case

When does Frau Grün use the genitive case? She uses it when the noun is the owner or possessor of something, e.g.

Das Kaninchen **des** Mannes ist hungrig.	The man's rabbit is hungry.
Der Hut **der** Frau ist groß.	The lady's hat is large.
Die Farbe **des** Hauses ist schrecklich.	The colour of the house is terrible.
Die Bücher **der** Kinder sind alt.	The children's books are old.

There are also a few prepositions which are followed by the genitive case.

The dative case

When does Frau Grün use the dative case? She uses it when the noun is the indirect object of the verb, or after certain prepositions. In English, if you say, *The teacher gives the girl the book*, the object that the teacher (nominative) is giving, is the book (accusative). She is giving it **to** the girl, so the girl is called the indirect object and in German you have to use the dative case.

When Frau Grün has items in both the dative and the accusative case she **always** picks the dative items first, e.g.

| Die Lehrerin gibt **dem** Mädchen das Buch. | The teacher gives the girl the book. |

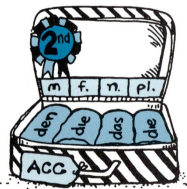

3 Adjectives

Adjectives are words which describe nouns, e.g. red, huge, stupid, etc. When you are writing German, you've no doubt noticed that adjectives seem to have a nasty habit of changing their endings according to which form of **der**, **ein** or **kein** you are using.

(There are other words which also affect the ending, but tackle these ones first as they are the most useful.)

The agreeable Grüns – The Grüns are very fussy about their appearance. They like clothes which go together, or which agree with each other. Getting words to agree means that they have to have the right ending according to their gender, case and whether they are singular or plural, e.g.

Der Hund ist auf **dem** Tisch. → **Der** durstige Hund ist auf **dem** klein**en** Tisch.

Other words which behave like **der**, **die** and **das** include **dies(er)** (= this), **jed(er)** (= each) and **welch(er)** (= which).

Demonstrative adjectives

These are the endings which Frau Grün picks out to go with:

dies-	this
jed-	each, every
welch-	which

Before you groan at yet another set of endings, look back at the **der**, **die**, **das** chest. Notice anything? The endings are the same, apart from the neuter singular nominative and accusative, so there really isn't much extra to learn.

| Welch**er** Hund ist auf dies**em** Tisch? | Which dog is on this table? |

If you liven things up with an adjective or two, you treat **welcher** and **dieser** like **der** words, e.g.

| Welch**er** durstige Hund ist auf dies**em** klein**en** Tisch? | Which thirsty dog is on this small table? |
| Diese jung**en** Frauen wohn**en** in dies**en** klein**en** Häusern. | These young women live in these small houses. |

Obviously it is better to be accurate if you can, but don't worry too much about getting the endings right, particularly if you are taking the Foundation Level.

In reading and listening exams it is very important that you make your meaning clear, and you will not be penalised for minor grammatical mistakes.

By the time you come to the exam, you will be using many expressions automatically, and you will get the endings and cases right without consciously thinking about them.

Using ein or kein

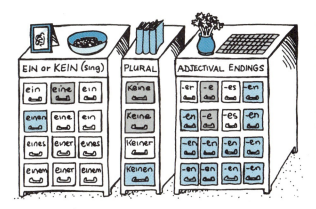

Frau Grün finds outfits with **ein** (= a) or **kein** (= not a) rather plain, so she dresses up the adjectives with a selection of endings, e.g.

| Ein Hund ist auf einem Tisch. | A dog is on a table. |
| Ein durstig**er** Hund ist auf einem klein**en** Tisch. | A thirsty dog is on a small table. |

Look at the two sets of chests of drawers, and you will see that the grey drawers are the same in both sets – same place for the same **-en** endings. The blue drawers are easy – all end in **-e**, so that only leaves you with five to remember. Don't try to learn all these rules in one go, but use them to refer to from time to time. They may help you to make more sense of what you are learning.

During your GCSE course, you will find yourself meeting many useful sentences and phrases. As long as you get them to agree, you can ring the changes on a fairly limited number of expressions and amaze everyone with what appears to be your vast knowledge.

A sneaky tip

As long as you keep an adjective and its noun separate, you don't have to put a special ending on the adjective to make it agree with its noun.

If you can't manage,

| Es gibt einen gut**en** Film im Kino. | There is a good film at the cinema. |

say,

| Der Film im Kino ist gut. | The film at the cinema is good. |

The gets you out of having to remember the right ending for **gut**.

4 Adverbs

These are words which describe verbs, e.g. *quickly, carelessly, badly.*

The Müller family does everything quickly, carelessly or badly and, as you can imagine, they are none too concerned about their appearance and certainly can't be bothered to worry about things agreeing. Therefore, every time they use adverbs, they don't bother with a special ending, e.g.

| Der Zug fährt schnell. | The train goes quickly. |
| Marlene singt laut. | Marlene sings loudly. |

5 Adjectives:
comparative / superlative

When you want to compare two things, e.g. a *bigger* hat, a *taller* man, take the adjective and add **-er** to it, just as you do in English, except, of course, remember that Frau Grün adds something extra to make everything agree. Also, she can't resist umlauts, so she usually adds one to the adjective if it originally was a single syllable word with an **a**, **o**, or **u** as its vowel.

This is called the comparative form of the adjective.

| eine große Katze | a big cat |
| eine größere Katze | a bigger cat |

- With some adjectives there is a slight change or the addition of an umlaut in the spelling:

teuer → teurer	dear → dearer
dunkel → dunkler	dark → darker
groß → größer	large → larger

When you want to compare three or more things, you need a superlative form of the adjective. Take the adjective and add **-ste**, plus the appropriate ending and an umlaut where possible, e.g.

Adjective	*Comparative*	*Superlative*
schnell	schneller	der / die / das schnell**ste**
warm	w**ä**rmer	der / die / das wärm**ste**
klein	kleiner	der / die / das klein**ste**
arm	**ä**rmer	der / die / das **ä**rm**ste**

der warme Mantel	the warm coat
Der Mantel von Gabi / Gabis Mantel ist warm, aber der Mantel von Marlene / Marlenes Mantel ist wärmer.	Gabi's coat is warm, but Marlene's coat is warmer.
Lotte Marx, aber hat den wärmsten Mantel.	Lotte Marx has the warmest coat.

or

Der Mantel von Lotte ist der wärmste.

There are, naturally, some irregular forms, but you don't need to make a special effort to learn them for GCSE. The most common is probably **gut**, but, conveniently for English speakers, the German equivalent of *good – better – best*, is:
gut – besser – (das) beste

5 Adverbs:
comparative / superlative

These could not be easier, since you add **-er** to the adverb to form the comparative – just as you do in English, e.g.

| Anna läuft schnell, aber Maria läuft schneller. | Anna runs fast, but Maria runs faster. |

To run the *fastest*, or do something *the best*, the superlative adverb, you take the superlative adjective and add **-en**; in front of this word you write **am**, e.g.

Hugo fährt schnell.	Hugo drives fast.
Klaus fährt schneller.	Klaus drives faster.
Rudi fährt am schnellsten.	Rudi drives the fastest.

When you want to compare ways in which things are done, you will need comparative or superlative adverbs.

 Good news!
You form comparative adverbs in the same way as you do comparative adjectives, so there's nothing new to learn here! To form a superlative adverb, you often add **-sten** to the adjective and write **am** in front.

 Even better news!
Comparative and superlative adverbs keep the same ending, so you don't have to think about cases or genders – for once!

Adjective	*Comparative*	*Superlative*
schnell	schneller	am schnellsten
langsam	langsamer	am langsamsten

Frau Grün fährt schnell.	Frau Grün drives fast.
Frau Müller fährt schneller.	Frau Müller drives faster.
Herr Marx fährt am schnellsten.	Herr Marx drives the fastest.

 Bad news
There are some irregular forms. Remember that if you like something you can say, **Ich habe... gern**, but if you prefer or like something else more you have to say, **Ich habe... lieber**.

The only irregular forms that you are likely to meet on a regular basis, are:
gern – lieber – am liebsten.

Gerhard spielt gern Geige.	Gerhard likes playing the violin.
Marlene tanzt lieber.	Marlene prefers dancing.
Martin spielt am liebsten Fußball.	Martin likes playing football best of all.

7 Prepositions

Prepositions are words which usually describe the place where something is, e.g. *in, on, beside, with*. The tidy-minded Frau Grün has pockets in the lids of her accusative, genitive and dative cases in to which she tucks her prepositions.

...always followed by the accusative case

... **always followed by the dative case**

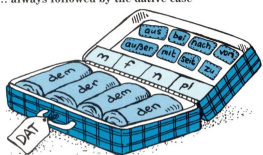

Gerhard fährt durch den Wald.	Gerhard goes through the wood.
Der Bahnhof ist um die Ecke.	The railway station is around the corner.
Marlene kauft ein Geschenk für ihren Freund / ihre Freundin.	Marlene is buying a present for her friend.

...always followed by the genitive case
The only ones you are likely to meet are **während** (= during), **trotz** (= in spite of) and **wegen** (= on account of). You will not meet them very often, so it is probably easier just to memorise an expression which you personally find useful.

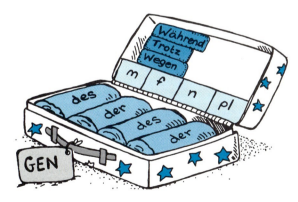

| Trotz des schönen Wetters blieben wir zu Hause. | In spite of the lovely weather, we stayed at home. |

Gerhard fährt mit dem Fahrad durch den Wald.	Gerhard goes through the wood on his bike.
Martin ist mit seiner Schwester einkaufen gegangen. Später hat er mit seinem Freund gespielt.	Martin went shopping with his sister. Later he played with his friend.
Gretchen hat einen Brief von ihrem Onkel und ihrer Tante bekommen.	Gretchen received a letter from her uncle and aunt.

...followed by either the accusative or the dative case
Frau Grün finds **auf** (= at, to, on), **in** (= in), **vor** (= in front of), **unter** (= under), **über** (= above) and **zwischen** (= between) so useful that she has pockets in two cases especially for them. She doesn't like being without them, so when she is travelling around, she uses the accusative case, and when she is staying in one place, she uses the dative case. E.g.

| Der Hund war im Wohnzimmer, als die Katze ins Zimmer lief. | The dog was in the living room when the cat ran in to the room. |
| Der Hund schlief auf dem Bett, als die Katze auf das Bett sprang. | The dog was asleep on the bed when the cat leapt on to the bed. |

Which is which?

Place and dative each have an **a** sound, so when the prepositions are stationary and stay in one place, they are followed by the dative. You can also remember a common expression like **ins Kino** which you use when you are going (in)to the cinema.

Ins is short for **in das**, and as **das** is accusative and not dative, it must be used for movement.

in	+ das =	ins
in von zu	+ dem =	im vom zum
zu	+ der =	zur

German Revision Guide

Ich gehe ins Kino.	I am going to the cinema.
Ich sitze im Garten.	I am sitting in the garden.
Ich gehe zum Bahnhof.	I am going to the station.
zum Beispiel	for example
Zur Zeit regnet es.	At present it is raining.

 Some verbs take preposition that aren't the same as those in English. E.g.

an (+ acc.)	denken an	to think about
	sich erinnern an	to remember about
	schreiben an	to write to
auf (+ acc.)	warten auf	to wait for
	sich freuen auf	to look forward to
um (+ acc.)	bitten um	to ask for

| in (+ dat.) | ankommen in | to arrive in / at |
| nach (+ dat.) | fragen nach | to ask about / make enquiries, e.g. price |

Which case?

- You needn't get too fussed about **während** (= during), **trotz** (= in spite of) or **wegen** (= because of): these are followed by the genitive case (remember WTW).
- You already know about **auf** (= at, to, on), **in** (= in), **vor** (= in front of), **unter** (= under), **über** (= above) and **zwischen** (= between).
- There are only five common prepositions followed by the accusative case: **durch** (= through), **für** (= for, because), **gegen** (= against), **ohne** (= without), **um** (=about).

Think of an 'accusing' finger.

- All the others which you may meet at GCSE level are likely to be followed by the dative, but if you want to learn them, or have them for reference, the most common are: **aus** (= out), **außer** (= besides), **gegenüber** (= opposite), **mit** (=with), **nach** (= towards, after), **seit** (= since), **von** (= from) and **zu** (= to).

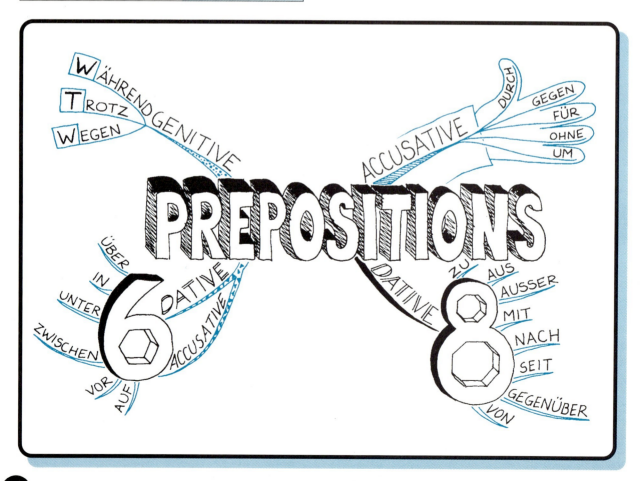

8 Verbs

Energy-saving infinitives – Frau Grün believes in saving energy. She has worked out that by learning one form of the verb – the infinitive – she can say how she can do, or wants to do, all manner of things, how things ought to be done, or how she has to do something.

She is also something of a fortune-teller, because she can talk knowledgeably about the future. Finally, by knowing or working out the infinitive, she can look up unknown verbs in a dictionary. Not a bad return for the little effort of learning one word form!

In English, the infinitive is the to-form of the verb, e.g. *to run, to have, to live*. German infinitives are single words ending in **-n** or **-en**, e.g. laufen (= to run), **haben** (= to have) and **wohnen** (= to live). You don't usually put **zu** (= to) in front of the verb, as you would in English.

Frau Grün is so proud of her skill with infinitives, that she always serves them at the end of a meal, i.e. at the end of a sentence.

The future with infinitives

Ingredients	Method
werden (= to become)	1 Prepare appropriate part of **werden**.
infinitive	2 Add infinitive of your choice.
	3 Serve with confidence.

To form the future tense in German, you simply take the appropriate part of **werden** (= to become), followed by the infinitive. e.g.

| Er wird gehen. | He will go. |
| Ich werde wohnen. | I will live. |

 Remember, the dessert is at the end of the meal, and Frau Grün saves the infinitive till the end!

Frau Grün's alternative – To ring the changes, Frau Grün sometimes uses the present tense of a verb with a *time marker*. This means that she doesn't have to use **werden**; all she needs to remember is that the *timemarker* is immediately followed by the verb.

Gerhard und Gretchen werden ihre Hausaufgaben machen.	Gerhard and Gretchen will do their homework.
Morgen machen Gerhard und Gretchen ihre Hausaufgaben.	Tomorrow Gerhard and Gretchen will do their homework.
Marlene wird ihre Taute besuchen.	Marlene will visist her aunt
Nächste Woche besucht Marlene ihre Tante.	Next week Marlene will visist her aunt.
Am Montag fährt Frau Grün in die Stadt.	On Monday Frau Grün will go into town.

Using a dictionary

If you want to look up a verb in a dictionary, you need its infinitive form. This can present problems if the verb form which you're using looks very different from its infinitive, so you might have to do some preliminary detective work – particularly when translating from German to English.

If you see what looks like an unfamiliar German verb, try making an intelligent guess as to its English equivalent and then look up the English version to see if you can spot any resemblance. If you are correct, not only will you have solved your immediate problem, but you might also remember the verb form to use yourself at some time.

Er fährt mit dem Bus. (= He goes by bus.)

The **er** (= he) form, the third person singular, ends in **-t**, and the infinitive will probably end in **-en**: try **fähren**. This isn't quite right, so try taking off the umlaut, because many verbs add one in the third person. Look up **fahren** and you will find *to go, to travel* or *to drive*, depending on which dictionary you have. *He goes by bus* is the translation, and you now know how to use **fahren** in the third person singular, present tense.

Sie fährt mit dem Auto. (= She is going by car.)

German Revision Guide

Mystery modals

Frau Grün always keeps lots of these words at hand; if you follow her example, you'll score top marks with the examiners.

The modal verbs are:
können	to be able to
mögen	to like to
wollen	to want to
sollen	to be supposed to
müssen	to have to
dürfen	to be allowed to

Here's how the infinitive and the modal verbs team up to create a brilliant mixture:

Gerhard Grün *möchte* lesen.	Gerhard Grün would like to read.
Marlene Müller *möchte* Popsängerin werden.	Marlene Müller would like to become a pop singer.
Martin Müller *will* seine Hausaufgaben nicht machen.	Martin Müller doesn't want to do his homework.
Martin Müller *soll* heute nicht fernsehen.	Martin Müller should not watch TV today.

Martin's modal magnets

You have already met modal verbs. Martin Müller has some fiendish modal magnets which have such a devastating effect on the infinitives that they send them scuttling to the end of the sentence or clause:

lesen	to read
Ich *kann* das Buch lesen.	I can / am able to read the book.
Ich *möchte* das Buch lesen.	I would like to read the book.
Er *will* das Buch lesen.	He wants to read the book.

 Remember: Er will (= he wants), er wird (= he will – *future*)

Feeling weak or strong?

Here are some lists of everyday German verbs which you may find helpful for reference. These are the ones which tend to be the most common, but feel free to add more if it would help you.

Group One – weak verbs
Infinitive or to-form = stem + **en**

Present	Imperfect	Perfect	Future
stem + ending	stem + ending	ge + stem + t	werden + inf.
(see page 139)	(see page 139)	(see page 141)	(see page 135)

Verbs which behave like this are called weak verbs.

Grammar

All examples, except for the infinitives themselves, are given in the third person singular (**er**, **sie** or **es** form).

Infinitive	Present	Imperfect	Perfect	
besuchen	besucht	besuchte	hat besucht	visit
erklären	erklärt	erklärte	hat erklärt	explain
erzählen	erzählt	erzählte	hat erzählt	tell
fragen	fragt	fragte	hat gefragt	ask
glauben	glaubt	glaubte	hat geglaubt	believe
hoffen	hofft	hoffte	hat gehofft	hope
kaufen	kauft	kaufte	hat gekauft	buy
kochen	kocht	kochte	hat gekocht	cook
machen	macht	machte	hat gemacht	make
öffnen	öffnet	öffnete	hat geöffnet	open
regnen	regnet	regnete	hat geregnet	rain
sagen	sagt	sagte	hat gesagt	say
sparen	spart	sparte	hat gespart	save money
spielen	spielt	spielte	hat gespielt	play
wohnen	wohnt	wohnte	hat gewohnt	live

All of the verbs in the first box are also known as regular verbs, because they keep the same stem throughout. A few common weak verbs are also irregular and change their stem.

brennen	brennt	brannte	hat gebrannt	burn
bringen	bringt	brachte	hat gebracht	bring
denken	denkt	dachte	hat gedacht	think
haben	hat	hatte	hat gehabt	have
kennen	kennt	kannte	hat gekannt	know – a person

Group Two – strong verbs

Strong verbs form their past tenses by slightly changing their stem, and by putting **-en** instead of **-t** at the end of their past participle.

Infinitive	Present	Imperfect	Perfect	
anfangen	fängt an	fing an	hat angefangen	begin
beginnen	beginnt	begann	hat begonnen	begin
bieten	bietet	bot	hat geboten	offer
bleiben	bleibt	blieb	ist geblieben	stay
essen	isst	aß	hat gegessen	eat
fahren	fährt	fuhr	ist gefahren	go, travel
finden	findet	fand	hat gefunden	find
geben	gibt	gab	hat gegeben	give
gehen	geht	ging	ist gegangen	go
helfen	hilft	half	hat geholfen	help
kommen	kommt	kam	ist gekommen	come
lesen	liest	las	hat gelesen	read
nehmen	nimmt	nahm	hat genommen	take
schlafen	schläft	schlief	hat geschlafen	sleep
schließen	schließt	schloß	hat geschlossen	shut
schneiden	schneidet	schnitt	hat geschnitten	cut
schwimmen	schwimmt	schwamm	hat / ist geschwommen	swim
sehen	sieht	sah	hat gesehen	see
sein	ist	war	ist gewesen	be
sprechen	spricht	sprach	hat gesprochen	speak
stehen	steht	stand	hat gestanden	stand
steigen	steigt	stieg	ist gestiegen	climb
tragen	trägt	trug	hat getragen	carry
tun	tut	tat	hat getan	do
vergessen	vergisst	vergaß	hat vergessen	forget

You'll find what you need about the perfect tense on page 141.

German Revision Guide

Reflexive verbs

In German, you sometimes have to say that you do something yourself, or to yourself.

Ich setze mich.	(= I sit (myself) down)
Ich wasche mich.	I have a wash.

This is how it works:

Ich setze mich.	I sit down.
Du setzt dich.	You sit down.
Er / sie / es setzt sich.	He / she / it sits down.
Wir setzen uns.	We sit down.
Ihr setzt euch.	You sit down.
Sie (formal) setzen sich.	You sit down.
Sie setzen sich.	They sit down.
Ich wasche mich.	I have a wash.
Du wäschst dich.	You have a wash.
Er / sie / es wäscht sich.	He / she / it has a wash.
Wir waschen uns.	We have a wash.
Ihr wascht euch.	You have a wash.
Sie (formal) waschen sich.	You have a wash.
Sie waschen sich.	They have a wash.

Imperatives and reflexives

In English you can choose whether to say, *Sit down* or, *Sit yourselves down*, but in German you must use the second version. This is how you do it.
Setz(e) dich!
Setzt euch!
Setzen Sie sich!

You probably won't need to order anyone about, but you might need to recognise commands.

Impersonal verbs

If you want to say *I like* in German, a very common way is to say that *it is pleasing to you*.

Es gefällt mir.	I like / it is pleasing to me.)

😊 **Good news**

By changing the pronoun, you can use the same expressions in sentences concerning other people, not just yourself, e.g.

Schach gefällt Gerhard.	Gerhard likes chess.
Filme gefallen seiner Mutter.	His mother likes films.

 It is pleasing to *me*, to *Gerhard*, to *his mother* – so they are all in the dative case.

You can also use an impersonal verb + dative, when something is wrong or you want to say that you're sorry.

Es tut mir weh.	It hurts.
Es tut mir Leid.	I'm sorry.

Passive verbs

If something is done to something, the verb is called a passive verb.

The door was opened, the cup was broken are English examples of passive verbs. Although the passive exists in German, you don't need to be able to form it for GCSE except in certain set expressions. If you want to use the idea of the passive, though, without learning the construction, there is an easy way round it by using **jemand**, someone.

Trust Martin Müller to blame someone else!

Jemand hat die Tür geöffnet.	The door was opened. / Someone opened the door.
Jemand hat die Tasse zerbrochen.	The cup was broken. / Someone broke the cup.

Grammar

9 Tenses

With a little help from Frau Grün, you can easily learn how to form different tenses in German when using regular verbs. (Regular verbs are those which follow the usual patterns.)

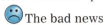 The bad news

Although most verbs are regular, in German as in English, you will find some that appear to do their own thing. After all, in English you say *bought*, *went*, *had*, and so on – and not 'buyed', 'goed', or 'haved'.

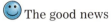 The good news

Irregular verbs which you will need for GCSE are so common that you will probably have been using them and getting them right for ages, without really thinking.

Ich bin (= I am) and **ich hatte** (= I had) are both examples of irregular verbs which you probably use automatically. Try to learn sentences and expressions which use these verbs, rather than to memorise them in long lists. If you are really keen to get your German spot on, try grouping them on Mind Maps or in other ways which work well for you.

Present

As you have already seen, Frau Grün is an expert with infinitives.

Sometimes, however, she likes to add a bit of variety to her recipe.

Ingredients	Method
one verb stem of your choice	1 Take suitable verb and strip down to its stem.
one appropriate ending	2 Change the middle if necessary.
	3 Add appropriate ending.
	4 Serve immediately.

Infinitive: **wohnen** (= to live)					
Stem: **wohn**					
ich	wohn	-e	wir	wohn	-en
du	wohn	-st	ihr	wohn	-t
			Sie	wohn	-en
er / sie / es	wohn	-t	sie	wohn	-en

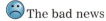 The bad news

Although most verbs work like **wohnen** in the present tense, there are some which seem to be a law unto themselves – or, as the grammar books say, are irregular.

 The good news

However, many of these are very common verbs which you will have been using for so long that you have probably learnt them already without realising it.

 Even better news

Other verbs like this are so rare that you won't need to know them for your GCSE.

Imperfect

In English, you say that you used to do something or that you were doing something; you have two different verb forms.

You will be pleased to know that German has only one way of saying both, and this is called the imperfect tense.

Frau Grün *used to make* imperfect pizzas, and *was practising* for a long time before she became a perfect cook. Judge for yourself her imperfect attempts.

Ingredients	Method
one verb stem	1 Take verb stem.
	2 Add appropriate ending.
one appropriate ending	3 Serve with confidence, because as you can see, the imperfect tense is very, very easy!

WOHNEN					
ich	wohn	-te	wir	wohn	-ten
du	wohn	-test	ihr	wohn	-tet
			Sie	wohn	-ten
er / sie / es	wohn	-te	sie	wohn	-ten

 Occasionally, Frau Grün likes to be unpredictable and serve up something which does not follow the pattern. Yes, it's one of those irregular verbs again.

SINGEN			
ich	sang	wir	sangen
du	sangst	ihr	sangt
		Sie	sangen
er / sie / es	sang	sie	sangen

SEIN			
ich	war	wir	waren
du	warst	ihr	wart
		Sie	waren
er / sie / es	war	sie	waren

11

German Revision Guide

Separable verbs

Frau Grün has a food processor with all sorts of different gadgets which she can attach to it to perform different tasks. In Frau Grün's store cupboard are useful little words which she tacks on to the front of a verb (i.e. gives it a prefix) to change its meaning.

These are the most useful of her prefixes:

ab (= off), **an** (= on), **auf** (= at, to), **aus** (= out, from), **ein** (= in), **um** (= around), **zu** (= to).

Often, but not always, the prefix combined with the verb which follows gives you a clue as to the meaning of the verb, e.g.

geben	to give	ausgeben	to spend – money, not time		
machen	to make	ausmachen	to switch off	zumachen	to close
steigen	to climb	aussteigen	get off	einsteigen	to get in
kommen	to come	ankommen	to arrive		
stehen	to stand	aufstehen	to get up		
fahren	to go, travel	abfahren	to depart	anfahren	to run into, to hit
holen	to fetch	abholen	to meet	überholen	to overtake
hören	to hear	zuhören	to listen		

...present and imperfect

Separable prefixes make complete words in themselves, and Frau Grün unclips them from the rest of the verb and puts them carefully at the end of the clause or sentence.

Gretchen macht die Tür **zu**.	Gretchen closes the door.
Marlene gibt zu viel Geld **aus**.	Marlene spends too much money.
Herr Müller kam um sieben Uhr **an**.	Herr Müller arrived at seven o'clock.

Frau Grün likes to use separable prefixes to give that extra something to her cooking.

Gretchen **geht** um sechs Uhr **aus**. (ausgehen = to go out)	Gretchen is going out at six o'clock.
Gerhard **kam** um drei Uhr **an**. (ankommen = to arrive)	Gerhard arrived at three o'clock.

...future

You'll be glad to know that there's nothing new here. You simply treat the verbs like any other infinitive.

Gabi wird morgen ankommen.	Gabi will arrive tomorrow.
Martin wird später aufstehen.	Martin will get up later.

...perfect

Frau Grün takes the usual past participle, e.g. **gekommen**, **gehört** and sticks the prefix on the front of it to make **angekommen**, **zugehört**.

Gerhard ist um halb zwei **ab**ge**fahren**.	Gerhard left at half past one.
Gretchen hat die Tür **zu**ge**macht**.	Gretchen shut the door.

More examples: zu → machen
ein → steigen
an → kommen

Grammar

Perfect

In English, you say *you did* or *have done* something.

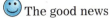 The good news
In German there is only one way of doing this, so you don't have to worry about learning two sets of rules.

Frau Grün's perfect sarnies

First she chooses a piece of **haben** or **sein** and then she chooses the appropriate past participle (the past participle in German, is often a **ge-** word; some examples of past participles are **gemacht** (= made), **gearbeitet** (= worked), **gegangen** (= gone), e.g.

Die Familie hat gewohnt.   The family lived /
                            The family has lived.

Gerhard ist gegangen.   Gerhard went /
                         Gerhard has gone.

However, sandwiches are not very exciting without a filling – they're jazzed up with extra information, e.g.

Die Familie hat in der   The family lived in
Stadt gewohnt.   the town.

Gretchen ist nach   Gretchen came home.
Hause gekommen.

Haben or sein?

Most verbs use **haben**; those that don't are **sein** (= to be), **werden** (= to become) and most, but not all of the verbs which are to do with *coming* and *going*.

Frau Grün **ist** in die   Frau Grün drove into
  Stadt **gefahren**.   town.
Am Montag **ist**   On Monday, Frau Grün
  Frau Grün in die   drove into town.
  Stadt **gefahren**.
Gerhard **hat** eine   Gerhard took a test.
  Prüfung **gemacht**.
Letzte Woche **hat**   Last week, Gerhard
  Gerhard eine   took a test.
  Prüfung **gemacht**.

Another sneaky tip

You can easily remember these two: **hin** (= away) and **her** (= towards). Remember **her** and *towards* both contain the letter r.
Ich gehe hinaus.   I am going out.
Ich bin hinausgegangen.   I went out.
Ich komme herein.   I am coming in.
Ich bin hereingekommen.   I came in.

Past participles

Frau Grün uses different kinds of bread (verbs) for her sandwiches. The most popular is **ge-t**; grammar books call these weak verbs. She also likes to use **ge-n**; grammar books call these strong verbs.

Finally, of course, you can't escape irregular verbs. These are easier to remember if you learn sentences containing the most common ones. It's also a good idea to learn any irregularities in new verbs as you go along, but you could also draw Mind Maps showing the different verb families.

Martin Müller's magnets are also very effective at splitting up verbs and their past participles.

Er hat gesehen.	He saw / has seen.
Er hat den Hund gesehen.	He saw / has seen the dog.
Er hat den Hund im Garten gesehen.	He saw / has seen the dog in the garden.
Heute hat er den Hund mit Marlene im Garten gesehen.	He saw the dog today in the garden with Marlene.

Inseparable verbs

Following a holiday in England, the Müllers have become addicted to fish and chips, without sauce – nothing either added or taken away. They tend to indulge in large helpings, leaving no room to add or change anything.

Most verbs form their past participles with **ge-**, but verbs which begin with **be-, ge-, ver-** are said to have inseparable prefixes, i.e. the letters on the front always go with the rest of the verb – just as fish and chips are never apart. Most of the time you don't need to bother about them, but when you form the past participle, remember the Müller's overloaded plates and you will have no room for an extra **ge-**.

That's just about all that you need to know about forming and recognising the perfect tense. Don't try to learn all the rules at once, but maybe now when you meet a sentence in the perfect tense, you will find it easier to understand how it has been put together, and by the time of the examination you too will be making perfect sandwiches!

10 Word order

More of Martin's magnets

Martin has special magnets which have a peculiar effect on verbs.

Martin war zu Hause. Er war krank.

Martin was at home. He was ill.

However, if you want to say in German that Martin was at home because he was ill, Martin's **weil** magnet repels the verb and sends it scuttling to the other end of the clause or sentence:

Martin war zu Hause, **weil** er krank **war**.

Gerhard sah Marlene. Gerhard kam nach Hause.

Gerhard saw Marlene. Gerhard came home.

Gerhard sah Marlene, **bevor** er nach Hause **kam**.

Gerhard saw Marlene before he came home.

Martin has one more trick up his sleeve. His verb magnet attracts other verbs if it is at the end of the clause, so the verb in the next part of the sentence is irresistibly attracted:

Als Marlene im Kino **war**, **sah** sie Gerhard.
Bevor Gretchen nach Hause **kam**, **sah** sie ihre Freundin.

Getting everything in order

Simple sentences and questions follow the same word order as they do in English. E.g.

Sie arbeitet in einem Laden.	She works in a shop.
Sie sind nicht da.	They are not there.
Bist du krank?	Are you ill?

Asking questions

Meet Martin's three destructive dachshunds: **Wann?**, **Wie?** and **Wo?** Martin loves letting them loose to play havoc with German word order where they act like magnets attracting, pulling and tugging at the verbs, etc.

Wo / Wohin? (= where / where to) likes a quiet life, and obediently sits just where you would expect, e.g.

	Wo / Wohin?
Frau Grün kommt	nach Hause.

Wie? (= how, in what manner) is rather pushy, and always barges in front of **Wo / Wohin?**, e.g.

	Wie?	Wo / Wohin?
Marlene und Martin fahren	mit dem Bus	ins Kino.
Herr Müller kam	mit der Bahn	nach Hause.

Now for the worst of the three, **Wann?** (= when); it is always 'me first' with this dog, e.g.

	Wann?	Wie?	Wo / Wohin?
Martin und Marlene fahren	um acht Uhr	mit dem Bus	ins Kino.
Herr Müller kam	um drei Uhr	mit der Bahn	nach Hause.

German Revision Guide

Basically, **Wann?** likes worrying away at verbs, so he has to have one right next to him, e.g.

Wann kommt er?	When is he coming?
Er kommt heute. / Heute kommt er.	He is coming today.
Wie kommt er?	How is he coming?
Er kommt mit dem Auto.	He is coming by car.
Wohin kommt er?	Where is he coming?
Er kommt nach München.	He is coming to Munich.

Remember: **Wann?**, **Wie?**, **Wo / Wohin?** can be explained as Time–Manner–Place (TMP).

	Wann? (time)	Wie? (manner)	Wo / Wohin? (place)
Onkel Peter kommt	heute	mit dem Auto	nach München.

or

Wann? (time)	Wie? (manner)	Wo / Wohin? (place)	
Heute kommt Onkel Peter	mit dem Auto	nach München.	

Wann?, **Wie?** and **Wo / Wohin?** are easily remembered as they are in alphabetical order.

More examples, this time with the perfect tense:

Frau Grün ist in die Stadt gefahren.	Frau Grün drove into town.
Wann ist Frau Grün in die Stadt gefahren?	When did Frau Grün drive into town?
Am Montag ist Frau Grün in die Stadt gefahren.	On Monday, Frau Grün drove into town.
Gerhard hat eine Prüfung gemacht.	Gerhard did an exam.
Wann hat Gerhard eine Prüfung gemacht?	When did Gerhard do an exam?
Letzte Woche hat Gerhard eine Prüfung gemacht.	Last week Gerhard did an exam.

Wann? Wie? Wo / Wohin?

The dachshunds like to annoy the Grün family while they are having their evening meal, and the dogs always arrive before the dessert / infinitives, e.g.

	Wann? (time)	Wie? (manner)	Wo / Wohin? (place)	Infinitive
Gerhard wird	am Wochenende	mit dem Fahrrad	aufs Land	fahren.

Wann?, **Wie?** and **Wo / Wohin?** also can't leave verbs alone and drag them out of their usual place to make a meal of them.

Wann kommst du nach Hause?	When are you coming home?
Wie ist das Wetter heute?	What's the weather like today?
Wo ist mein Buch?	Where is my book?
Wann gehst du ins Kino?	When are you going to the cinema?
Wie sagt man das?	How do you say that?
Wo ist das Schloss bitte?	Where is the castle, please?

Three more magnets

Martin's question magnets have an irresistible attraction for verbs.

Was machst du?	What are you doing?
Warum kommst du hierher?	Why do you come here?
Wer steht im Garten?	Who is standing in the garden?

Remember: **Wer?** (= who), **Wo?** (= where).

11 Conjunctions

Motorway junctions join roads together. Grammatical conjunctions join sentences or clauses together.

Some conjunctions, which you may see called 'co-ordinating' conjunctions, merely link together two or more sentences which are capable of standing alone. You need **und** (= and), **aber** (= but), **oder** (= or) and **denn** (= for).

The good news

These conjunctions have no effect on German word order, e.g.

| Martin war zu Hause. Marlene war in der Schule. | Martin was at home. Marlene was at school. |

Joining these together with **und** or **aber** you have,

Martin war zu Hause **und** / **aber** Marlene war in der Schule.

Some bad news

Other conjunctions, the 'subordinating' conjunctions, join a sentence with a clause, and these do affect the word order:

bevor (= before), **bis** (= until), **obwohl** (= although), **nachdem** (= after), **wenn** (= if, when, whenever) and **als** (= when).

 Be careful: **wenn** (= when, whenever) and **als** (= when, i.e. on one occasion in the past), and **wann?** (= when, if you are asking a question).

Wenn es regnet, wird Gabi ihren Schirm mitnehmen.	If it rains, Gabi will take her umbrella.
Bevor Marlene ihre Freundin anruft, muss sie ihre Hausaufgaben machen. Marlene muss ihre Hausaufgaben machen, bevor sie ihre Freundin anruft.	Before Marlene telephones her friend, she must do her homework.
Martin sieht fern, bis sein Vater nach Hause kommt. / Bis sein Vater nach Hause kommt, sieht Martin fern.	Martin is watching TV until his father gets home.

 Good news

You've already met this construction when Martin Müller showed you his **weil** magnet on page 143. All these subordinating conjunctions work in the same way as **weil**.

Mock exam

Exam hints

Doing exams can be a scary experience. Even if you've swallowed several dictionaries and your nightmares are in German, there's always the terrible fear of the unknown and the unpredictable.

People tell you to relax. Great trick if you can do it. To relax you need to feel confident, and to feel confident you need to know what you're doing. And this doesn't just mean working your way through the lives of Gerhard and Marlene, useful though they are in making you very good at German.

To do as well as you possibly can, you need to know about exam technique. This is where our Helpful Hints come in. Follow them, and you'll improve your performance and get a better grade.

How the exam works...
There are four parts to the exam: Speaking, Listening, Reading and Writing. Each part is divided into three sections – Foundation, Foundation / Higher and Higher. If you are being entered at Foundation Level, you do both the Foundation and the Foundation / Higher Level questions. Higher Level students do the Foundation / Higher and the Higher Level questions. (Confused? Read it again!).

See page 7 for information on what you have to score to get each grade.

Speaking

Before you take your Speaking Test, you will be given two role play cards (either one Foundation and one Foundation / Higher Level, or one Foundation / Higher and one Higher Level). You will then have about 15 minutes, with a dictionary, to prepare them.

In some role plays, there is a surprise element – shown by a symbol, e.g.!

If you are doing NEAB or MEG, you will be expected to give a presentation on a prepared topic immediately after the role plays. You can learn this off by heart, but need to be ready to answer questions on the topic afterwards.

The final part of the Speaking Test is the General Conversation. Your teacher will ask you questions on two or three topic areas.

Helpful Hints
1   Dictionary warning! Watch out! They slow you down, and it is important that you prepare as much of the role play as you can before you go in. Don't be a perfectionist – read through everything first and jot down phrases you already know on a piece of paper. (You may take the paper, but not the dictionary, into the exam). The dictionary is a last resort, as it is often hard to find the right word when you are given several alternatives.
2   *Surprise* element. Here you need to use your imagination. Think about the situation described and try to guess what you might have to say. When you are in the exam, your teacher will then ask you a *surprise* question, or will *unexpectedly* disagree with you. If you don't understand the first time, say **Wie, bitte?**, and you'll get another chance.
3   Remember, role plays are meant to be two-way conversations, and you must listen to what your teacher says before you answer or say your bit.
4   Make your answers as detailed as you can, and remember to show off what you know. Marks are awarded for content, good use of language (variety of tenses, vocabulary and grammatical structure), pronunciation and accuracy.

Listening

Some exam boards (e.g. NEAB and WJEC) allow you to use a bilingual dictionary for five minutes before and after the listening exam. (Ask your teacher if you're not sure.) This can be useful for making sure you understand the questions before you start, or for checking the meaning of words you've managed to jot down but don't recognise. But don't think it's a big advantage – five minutes is not long and you'll still need to make sure you know the Rubrics on page 93 before you start.

Helpful Hints
1. Don't panic – you do not have to understand every word to answer the questions, and you hear everything twice. You are given plenty of time to write your answer after the second playing.
2. Answer in the right language! Instructions will say clearly whether to answer in English or German. The right answer in the wrong language will get no marks!
3. Don't worry too much about spelling. As long as it's recognisable (and in the right language) you'll get the mark.
4. Notice how many marks are awarded for each question, and answer as fully as you can – but don't add things you're not sure about as you could spoil a perfectly good answer.

Reading

All examination boards allow you to use a dictionary in the Reading Test.

Helpful Hints
1. First, answer as many questions as you can without looking at the dictionary.
2. Look up headings and nouns (they start with a Capital Letter!) first.
3. Read the questions before the text. This will give you an idea of what to look for.
4. With longer passages, skim the text looking for key words. When you've found where the answer is, note down the words you understand and if they don't seem to make much sense, have an intelligent guess.
5. Don't spend too long on any one question. Pace yourself so that you have time to try all questions.

6. Notice how many marks are available for each question and make sure your answers are detailed enough.
7. Answer in the right language!

Writing

Again, everyone is allowed to use a dictionary.

Helpful Hints
1. Use the dictionary to help you to understand the questions.
2. Divide your time equally between the questions.
3. Make sure you put down everything that is asked for. You can lose a huge number of marks for missing things out. Tick off each individual task when you have completed it.
4. Do the entire test without using the dictionary first. Remember to use what you know. Think of the expressions you are confident with and get them in somehow. Never, ever write it in English first and try to translate it. You might want to check the odd word when you've finished, but unless you are a skilled dictionary-user, you'll probably make more mistakes than you would have done if you hadn't had a dictionary.
5. Don't waffle irrelevantly. Marks are awarded for answering the question, using a wide range of language (tenses, vocabulary, grammatical structures), and accuracy.

You should now be ready to have a go at our Mock Exam. **Viel Glück!**

12

German Revision Guide

Speaking

You'll find the Speaking and Listening parts of the Mock Exam on Side 2 of the cassette. Remember, you do two role plays and have 15 minutes to prepare them, with a dictionary.

1 You are telling a German friend about where you live. Your teacher will play the part of your friend and will start the conversation. Say:
   a) you live in a house;
   b) there are six rooms and a garden;
   c) you have a car, but there's no garage;
   d) you like it.

Teacher's part:	Wo wohnst du?
	Wie groß ist dein Haus?
	Habt ihr ein Auto?
	Wie findest du dein Haus?

2 Your German penfriend's mother / father asks you about your part-time job. Your teacher will play the part of the mother / father and will start the conversation. Tell him / her:
   a) you work in a supermarket on Saturdays;
   b) you work from 10 till 2;
   c) you get £2.50 an hour;
   d) you walk there, and it takes 15 minutes;
   e) it's boring, but you need the money.

Teacher's part:	Hast du einen Job?
	Wie viele Stunden arbeitest du pro Tag?
	Wie viel Geld verdienst du?
	Wie kommst du dahin?
	Wie findest du die Arbeit?

3 Your German friend's mother / father is working in the kitchen and you'd like to help. Ask if you can help, say what you could do, how you normally help round the house and how much pocket money you get.

Your teacher will play the part of the mother / father and is using the polite *Sie*.
   a) Frag, ob du helfen kannst.
   b) Sag, was du machen könntest.
   c) Sag, wie du normalerweise zu Hause hilfst.
   d) Sag, wie viel Geld deine Eltern dir geben.

Teacher's part:	Ja, was machen Sie also?
	Gute Idee. Wie helfen Sie normalerweise zu Hause?
	Ach so. Bekommen Sie Geld dafür?

Listening

Foundation Level questions come first, so if you're doing Higher Level, you'll need to fast forward to the Foundation / Higher part before you start.

4 Stefan und Marina besprechen zwei Lehrer. Hör den Dialog an und füll die Lücken aus. Ist das Frau Smith oder Herr Wenzke?
   a) .... unterrichtet Englisch.   (1)
   b) .... ist streng.   (1)
   c) .... gefällt Marina und Stefan.   (1)
   d) .... ist manchmal sympathisch.   (1)

5 Wie kommt man am besten zur Post? Hör zu. Was ist richtig?   (1)

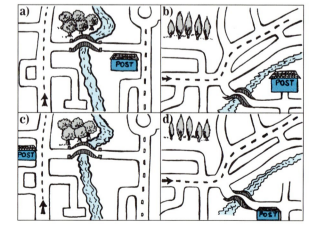

6 Heidi und Christiane machen Pläne für eine Campingreise. Hör zu. Was hat der Campingplatz? Markiere mit einem X. (5)

Der Campingplatz hat...

7 Die Wettervorhersage.

Wie wird das Wetter in Deutschland sein? Schreib die richtigen Buchstaben auf. (5)
Nord- und Westdeutschland: _____
Süddeutschland: _____

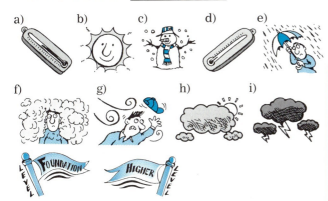

Beantworte die folgenden Fragen auf Deutsch.

8 In einem Geschäft.
Hör den Dialog an und beantworte die Fragen.
a) Was hat Fritz gekauft? (1)
b) Was ist das Problem? (1)
c) Was muß er jetzt kaufen? (1)

9 Josef Schiffer beschreibt seine neue Wohnung. Hör zu.
Beantworte die Fragen!
a) Wo ist Josefs Wohnung? (2)
b) Wie viele Zimmer hat die Wohnung? (1)
c) Was macht Josef, wenn er nicht einschlafen kann? (1)

Beantworte die folgenden Fragen auf Deutsch.

10 Petra spricht über ihre Schule. Hör zu und füll die Lücken aus.
a) Petras Schule ist ein .... (2)
b) Sie findet die Schule ...., denn fast alle wollen .... und sind .... (3)
c) Es kann schwer sein, wenn man .... finden will. (1)
d) Am .... hat Petra einen sympathischen .... kennen gelernt. (2)
e) Am Samstagabend haben sie .... gesehen. (1)

11 Jürgen beschreibt seine Ferien. Hör zu und beantworte die Fragen.
a) Was wollte Jürgens Vater jeden Tag machen? (2)
b) Warum hat das Jürgen nicht gern gemacht? (1)
c) Mit wem möchte Jürgen Ferien machen? (1)

Answers

1 a) Ich wohne in einem Haus.
  b) Es hat sechs Zimmer und einen Garten.
  c) Ja (wir haben ein Auto), aber keine Garage.
  d) Es gefällt mir gut.
2 a) Ich arbeite am Samstag in einem Supermarkt.
  b) Ich arbeite von 10 bis 14 Uhr / 2 Uhr.
  c) Ich bekomme / verdiene 2 Pfund 50 pro Stunde.
  d) Ich gehe zu Fuß. Es dauert 15 Minuten.
  e) Es ist langweilig, aber ich brauche das Geld.
3 (model answer)
  a) Kann ich Ihnen helfen?
  b) Ich könnte abspülen.
  c) Normalerweise gehe ich mit dem Hund spazieren.
  d) Ich bekomme zehn Pfund Taschengeld pro Woche.
4 a) Frau Smith; b) Herr Wenzke;
  c) Frau Smith; d) Herr Wenzke.
5 b.
6 a) X, b) X, c) –, d) –, e) X.
7 e); b).
8 a) einen Fotoapparat.
  b) Er funktioniert nicht.
  c) Batterien.
9 a) Fünf Minuten vom Bahnhof (1) und in der Nähe von einem guten Supermarkt (1);
  b) 4;
  c) Er sieht fern.
10 a) Gymnasium (1) für Mädchen (1);
   b) toll / sehr gut; lernen; freundlich;
   c) einen Freund;
   d) Freitag; Jungen;
   e) einen Film.
11 a) mindestens 15 Kilometer (1) wandern (1);
   b) das Wetter war zu heiß;
   c) mit einer Gruppe Freunde.

149

German Revision Guide

Answer the following questions in English.

12 Elke is talking about a road accident she was involved in last week. Listen to the cassette and then answer the following questions:
   a) Where exactly was Sabine when the accident took place? (1)
   b) What were the road conditions like? (2)
   c) Why did the accident happen? (1)
   d) What happened to the little boy? (3)
   e) How does Sabine feel about this? (2)

13 Christiane is looking for a birthday present for her boyfriend, Frank. She asks her friend Katrin for advice. Listen to the cassette and answer the following questions:
   a) What sort of present does Katrin suggest, and why? (2)
   b) What is Christiane's objection to the idea? (2)
   c) What do you think of Katrin's last suggestion, and why? (2)

Reading

14 In der Zeitung

> Beates Restaurant (Nähe Flughafen) sucht Kellner(in) mit Englisch und/oder Französisch.
> Montags bis Freitags 16 bis 23 Uhr.
> Wochenendarbeit auch möglich.
> Guter Lohn.
> Rufen Sie uns sofort an!
> Tel: 87 56 09

Was ist richtig? Markiere mit einem X.

a) Wo ist Beates Restaurant? (1)

b) Das Restaurant sucht (1)

c) Die Arbeit ist (1)
   i) am Mittag ☐   ii) am Abend ☐

d) Man muss

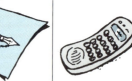

15 Bei der Reinigung

Pulli	1.40
Hose	8.90
Rock	8.90
Jacke	11.90
Kleid	11.90
Mantel	19.90

a) Schreib die richtige Nummer auf.

Was kostet DM19.90? ___ (1)

i) ii) iv) v) vi)
iii)

b) Was kostet ein Anzug? DM ___ (1)

Answers

12 a) on the bus;
b) quite wet (1) and busy (1);
c) boy didn't see the bus;
d) knocked down (1), broke his leg (1) and taken to hospital (1);
e) relieved (1) that it wasn't more serious (1).

13 a) box of chocolates – she knows a good shop nearby;
b) Frank has problems with his teeth and is trying to avoid sweet things;
c) good idea – he can eat the chocolates and then clean his teeth straight away / stupid idea – no one wants a toothpaste or a toothbrush for their birthday / it would still be bad for his teeth.

14 a) i; **b)** ii; **c)** ii; **d)** ii.
15 a) i; **b)** 20.80.

16 Beantworte diese Frage auf Deutsch.

Gaststätte Karl und Inge – Speisekarte

Vorspeisen	DM
Fleischsalat	7,50
Gemüsesuppe mit Brot	7,00
Krabbencocktail	8,50
Hauptgerichte	
Rinderbraten mit Pommes frites und Salat	15,00
Jägerschnitzel vom Schwein mit Kartoffeln und Gemüse	13,50
Lachs, in Butter gebraten, mit neuen Kartoffeln und Salat	16,50
Zum Nachtisch	
Schwarzwälderkirschtorte	6,00
Warmer Apfelstrudel	5,50
Käsekuchen	5,50
Getränke	
Wein (weiß od. rot)	2,00
Bier	2,50
Fruchtsaft	2,50

Bedienung nicht einbegriffen.

a) Frank ist Vegetarier. Was kann er als Vorspeise essen? (1)
b) Gisela isst sehr gern Fisch. Was kann sie zum Hauptgericht essen? (1)
c) Thorsten trinkt keinen Alkohol. Was kann er trinken? (1)
d) Karl ist allergisch gegen Milchprodukte. Was kann er nicht essen? (1)

17 Answer this question in English.

You receive this letter from your German penfriend.

> Vielen Dank für deinen letzten Brief und die Fotos von deiner Familie. Dein Bruder sieht gut aus! Deine Katze ist auch sehr süß. Wie alt ist sie jetzt?
>
> Im Moment habe ich leider keine Familienbilder für dich, aber ich schicke dir eine schöne Postkarte von meiner Stadt. An der linken Seite, neben der Kirche, steht meine Schule! Unser Haus ist dahinter, aber das siehst du nicht. Es ist sehr praktisch, in der Nähe von der Schule zu wohnen. Ich kann zu Fuß gehen und es dauert nur 3 Minuten! Wie kommst du zur Schule?
>
> Schreib bald!
>
> Deine Freundin Silke

a) What two things does Silke thank you for? (2)
b) What does she think of your brother? (1)
c) Where is her school? (1)
d) What two questions does she ask? (2)

18 Brieffreunde gesucht!

Wer hat diese Hobbys? Schreib den richtigen Namen.

> Ich suche Brieffreundschaften im Alter von 11 bis 13 Jahren. Meine Hobbys sind: Fußball spielen, Fotografieren und Malen. Schreibt mit oder ohne Foto an: Tanja Fischer, Alsenstr. 19, 67808 Imsweller.

> Ich bin 11 Jahre alt und suche nette Brieffreundinnen. Hobbys: Briefmarken sammeln, Federball und Malen. Jeder Brief wird beantwortet.
> Anna Meyer, Bogenstr. 4, 85012 Rosstal-Buffendorf.

> Hallo, ich suche Brieffreunde/innen aus Spanien und Frankreich. Bin 14 Jahre alt, spreche und schreibe Spanisch, Französisch und Deutsch. Meine Hobbys: Lesen, Musik hören und Briefe schreiben.
> Paula Kaufmann, Heidenstr. 45, 29229 Celle.

> Ich bin 13 Jahre alt und suche neue Brieffreunde/innen zwischen 12 und 14 Jahren. Hobbys: Schwimmen, Reiten, Musik hören, Klavier spielen und Computer spielen.
> Monika Schuhmacher, Eichenstr. 56, 77933 Lahr.

Answers

16 a) Gemüsesuppe; **b)** Lachs; **c)** Fruchtsaft; **d)** Käsekuchen.
17 a) letter and photos of family; **b)** goodlooking; **c)** next to the church; **d)** How old is your cat? How do you get to school?

Ich bin 11 Jahre alt und suche Brieffreundschaften von 10 bis 13 Jahren. Meine Hobbys: Schwimmen, Handball, Tanzen und Schlittschuh laufen.

Martina Schneider, Weisenstr. 3, 31157 Giften.

Name
.... (1)
.... (1)
.... (1)
.... (1)
.... (1)

19 Beantworte diese Frage *auf Deutsch*.

Lies diese Zusammenfassung von einem neuen Buch für Jugendliche, und dann füll die Lücken aus:

„Peters Idee" ist ein neues Buch für Jugendliche, die sich manchmal frustriert mit dem Leben fühlen.

Peter ist ein fünfzehnjähriger Junge, der gern Fußball spielt. Er sieht gut aus und hat viele Freunde und Freundinnen. Er versteht sich sehr gut mit seinen Eltern und darf fast alles machen, was er will.

Doch plötzlich verändert sich sein ganzes Leben. Seine Eltern werden in einem Straßenunfall schwer verletzt und müssen monatelang im Krankenhaus bleiben. Peter muss jetzt zu seiner Großmutter in den Schwarzwald ...

a) Peters Idee ist ein Roman für ... Leute. (1)
b) Peter ist ... und ... . (2)
c) Peter mag ... . (1)
d) Seine Eltern sind nicht zu ... mit ihm. (1)
e) Er muss zum ... umziehen, weil seine Eltern im ... sind. (2)

Beantworte die folgenden Fragen *auf Deutsch*.

20 Du bekommst einen kurzen Brief aus Deutschland.

Hallo Chris!
Wie geht's? Mir geht's im Moment nicht sehr gut. Ich habe zu viel Arbeit und nicht genug Freizeit! In zwei Wochen haben wir Prüfungen in der Schule und ich muss dafür büffeln. Hoffentlich bekomme ich gute Noten, aber ich bin sehr nervös!

Meine Eltern verstehen nicht, dass ich so wenig Zeit habe, und bestehen darauf, dass ich jeden Abend den Tisch decke, abspüle, und mit dem Hund spazieren gehe. Wenn ich das nicht mache, kriege ich kein Taschengeld! Das Leben ist so unfair!

Schreib bald, und sag mir, ob deine Eltern so gemein wie meine sind!
Dein Theo.

Richtig, falsch, oder nicht im Text?
a) Theo findet die Schule ziemlich wichtig. (1)
b) Er hat Angst vor den Prüfungen. (1)
c) Theo muss jeden Tag abwaschen, sonst bekommt er kein Taschengeld. (1)
d) Er mag den Hund nicht. (1)
e) Theo meint, es sei unfair, wenn Kinder zu Hause helfen müssen. (1)

21 Lies diesen Artikel aus einer deutschen Zeitschrift und beantworte die Fragen.

Du bist, was du isst!

Ernährst du dich gesund? Michaela, 15 Jahre, sagt uns, was sie von gesunder Ernährung hält:

'Ja, ich ernähre mich gesund, denn meine Eltern interessieren sich sehr für gesundes Essen. Mein Vater sagt, dass das Frühstück die wichtigste Mahlzeit ist, also frühstücken wir jeden Morgen zusammen.

In der Pause esse ich immer leckere Sachen, zum Beispiel Brot mit Hüttenkäse, Karotten und Rosinen.

> Wenn ich am Mittag aus der Schule komme, gibt es bei uns etwas Warmes zu essen. Meine Mutter kocht viel Vegetarisches und fast immer mit Olivenöl. Also ich denke, das ist sehr gesund.
>
> Abends esse ich, was ich will. Manchmal kaufe ich etwas Süßes oder Pommes frites, wenn ich mit Freunden in der Stadt bin, aber danach fühle ich mich immer schlecht, also versuche ich, meistens gesund zu essen.

Richtig oder Falsch?
a) Michaela frühstückt immer mit ihren Eltern.
b) Ihr Pausenbrot schmeckt gut.
c) Ihre Mutter kocht viel Fleisch, weil sie keine Vegetarierin ist.
d) Michaela findet es gut, manchmal ungesund zu essen. (4)

22 Lotte schreibt über ihr Lieblingshobby: Einkaufen. Lies den Text und finde die Wörter, die fehlen. Sieh dir die Wörterliste unten an.

> In meiner Stadt gibt es viele (a): die Bäckerei, die Metzgerei, die Apotheke, der Supermarkt, die Drogerie und viele Boutiquen. In meiner Stadt machen die Geschäfte um 9 Uhr auf und sie (b) um halb sechs. Sonntags haben sie (c) zu.
>
> Wenn ich (d) Geld habe, fahre ich samstagmorgens mit meiner Freundin in die Stadt. Wir gehen zum Einkaufszentrum.
>
> Meine Lieblingsboutique heißt *The Clothes Line*. Sie ist toll – sie hat immer die neueste (e) und ist nicht zu teuer. Ich kaufe gern Jeans und T-Shirts, weil sie sehr (f) sind. Letzten Samstag habe ich eine tolle grüne Hose und eine schwarze Jacke gekauft. Sehr schön – und sehr (g)!

a) Geschäfte   d) _____   g) _____
b) _____   e) _____
c) _____   f) _____

Mode	öffnen	Geschäfte	teuer
bequem	billig	nie	Musik
meistens	schließen	genug	wenig

23 Answer this question in English.

You receive this letter from your German penfriend:

> Hallo!
> Mir ist was schreckliches passiert! Mein Geldbeutel ist in einem Restaurant gestohlen worden. Ich bin am Samstag nachmittag mit einer Freundin aus der Schule einkaufen gegangen. Wir haben ziemlich viel gekauft – Kleidung, Musik u.s.w. und danach waren wir sehr hungrig und sind in ein Restaurant gegangen.
>
> Es war dumm, aber ich habe den Geldbeutel in meiner Manteltasche gelassen. Als wir zahlen wollten, war er verschwunden! Ich habe überall gesucht. Es war sehr peinlich, weil Sabine für mich zahlen musste, und sie bekommt relativ wenig Taschengeld. Ich bin sicher, dass der Kellner ihn genommen hat. Er sah sehr verdächtig aus. Aber ich hatte keine Beweise. Und 100 Mark waren darin! 5 Wochen Taschengeld!
>
> Hoffentlich hattest du ein besseres Wochenende als ich. Schreib bald!
> Deine Christiane.

a) What does Christiane think happened to her purse? (2)
b) Who is Sabine? (2)
c) What does Christiane regret doing? (1)
d) Why was she particularly embarrassed? (2)
e) What did she think of the waiter? (2)

Answers

18 stamp-collecting Anna; horse-riding Monika; letter-writing Paula; photography Tanja; iceskating Martina.
19 a) junge; **b)** fünfzehn, gutaussehend; **c)** Fußball (spielen); **d)** streng; **e)** Schwarzwald, Krankenhaus.
20 a) Richtig; **b)** Richtig; **c)** Richtig; **d)** Nicht im Text; **e)** Falsch.
21 a) Richtig; **b)** Richtig; **c)** Falsch; **d)** Falsch.
22 b) schließen; **c)** meistens; **d)** genug; **e)** Mode; **f)** bequem; **g)** billig.
23 a) It was stolen in a restaurant.
b) A friend from school.
c) Leaving her purse in her coat pocket.
d) Sabine had to pay for her, and she doesn't get much pocket money.
e) He looked suspicious, but she didn't have any proof that he'd stolen the purse.

12 Writing

FOUNDATION LEVEL

24 You are planning a meal with a German friend, who has offered to do the shopping while you are at school. Write a list in German, including six of the following types of food and drink:

25 An Austrian friend is staying in your area for a few days and you said you'd organise an evening out. Write a short note saying where you're going, when and where you're meeting, and how you're getting there. Don't forget to say 'bye at the end.

FOUNDATION / HIGHER LEVEL

26 Schreib einen Bericht über deine Schule.
Sag
...wie viele Schüler(innen) es gibt;
...was deine Lieblingsfächer sind.
Beschreib
...einen Lehrer oder eine Lehrerin;
...einen typischen Schultag.
Schreib deine Meinung über
... die Uniform;
... die Sportmöglichkeiten.

27 Du bist in den Ferien mit deiner Familie. Schreib eine Postkarte an deinen deutschen Brieffreund, Frank.
Sag ihm...
wo du bist;
mit wem;
wie das Wetter ist;
wie du das Hotel und das Essen findest, und warum;
was du heute zu Mittag gegessen hast;
was du gestern gemacht hast;
wie du die Ferien findest.

Answers

24 *(model answer)* Schinken, Käse, Karotten, Cola, Joghurt, Bananen.

25 *(model answer)* Wir gehen heute abend ins Kino. Wir treffen uns um halb acht vor dem Hotel. Wir fahren mit dem Bus. Tschüs!

26 *(model answer)* Ich besuche eine ziemlich große gemischte Gesamtschule. Es gibt ungefähr tausend Schüler(innen). Meine Lieblingsfächer sind Mathe und Physik, denn ich finde sie einfach und interessant. Mein Mathelehrerin heißt Frau Brown. Sie ist klein und schlank und hat kurze, lockige Haare. Sie ist nett, freundlich und sehr hilfsbereit. Montags stehe ich um halb acht auf, frühstücke, wasche mich, putze mir die Zähne und ziehe mich an. Ich fahre mit dem Bus zur Schule. Die Schule beginnt um 8 Uhr 45 und ist um 3 Uhr 25 aus. Wir haben fünf Stunden pro Tag, eine Pause und eine Mittagspause. Nach der Schule essen wir zu Abend, und dann mache ich meine Hausaufgaben. Danach sehe ich fern. Ich gehe um 10 Uhr 30 ins Bett.
In meiner Schule kann man viel Sport treiben. Es gibt einen Sportplatz, Tennisplätze und eine Turnhalle. In der Mittagspause kann man Federball oder Fußball spielen.
Wir müssen leider eine Schuluniform tragen: ein weißes Hemd, eine schwarze Hose oder einen schwarzen Rock, eine graue Jacke und eine gestreifte Krawatte. Das finde ich sehr langweilig.

27 *(model answer)* Hallo Frank! Ich bin mit meinen Eltern und meinem Bruder in Frankreich. Das Wetter ist warm und sonnig. Gestern bin ich im Meer geschwommen, aber es war ziemlich kalt. Das Hotel ist toll, denn es ist sehr bequem und es gibt ein gutes Restaurant. Das Essen ist lecker – ich habe heute zu Mittag Lachs mit Pommes gegessen. Ich finde die Ferien prima!
Tschüs! Dein(e)...

Sag ihm auch…
seit wann du hier bist;
was für Leute du hier kennengelernt hast;
was du morgen machen möchtest.

28 Du hast eine Tasche verloren, aber du weißt nicht, wo. Du warst letzte Woche bei einer deutschen Freundin. Schreib ihr einen Brief, und
…bedanke dich für den Aufenthalt;
sag
…was du verloren hast;
…wie die Tasche aussieht, und was darin war;
…wo die Tasche sein könnte;
…warum es ein Problem ist.

29 Schreib einen Brief an einen deutschen Brieffreund, und sag ihm
– wie du normalerweise zu Hause hilfst;
– wie du letztes Wochenende geholfen hast;
– wie viel Taschengeld du dafür bekommst;
– was du davon kaufst;
– wer bei dir was macht;
– ob du genug Taschengeld bekommst.

Mock exam

Answers

Hallo Frank! Ich bin seit drei Tagen mit meinen Eltern und meinem älteren Bruder in Frankreich. Das Wetter ist meistens schön, aber gestern hat es am Nachmittag geregnet. Am Morgen bin ich im Meer geschwommen, aber es war leider nicht besonders warm. Das Hotel gefällt mir wirklich gut, weil die Zimmer groß und bequem sind und es gibt ein Restaurant, wo man sehr gut essen kann. Ich habe heute zu Mittag Lachs mit Pommes gegessen – das ist mein Lieblingsfisch!
Die Leute sind hier sehr freundlich und ich habe vor zwei Tagen ein nettes Mädchen kennengelernt. Morgen abend möchten wir in die Disco gehen! Ich werde meine neue Lederjacke tragen.
Die Ferien sind echt gut!
Dein(e)…

28 *(model answer)* Hallo! Letzte Woche war toll! Es hat viel Spaß gemacht – danke für alles. Hast du vielleicht meine schwarze Sporttasche gefunden? Ich habe sie verloren, aber ich weiß nicht, wo. Sie ist ziemlich groß und meine Sportschuhe, Socken, ein weißes T-Shirt und weiße Shorts sind darin. Ich glaube, sie ist vielleicht im Kleiderschrank oder unter dem Bett. Mein Problem ist, ich möchte Tennis spielen! Aber ich kann es nicht, denn ich habe keine Sportschuhe! Hoffentlich hast du meine Tasche. Schreib bald! Dein Chris.

29 *(model answer)* Hallo Rolf! Normalerweise helfe ich nicht viel zu Hause, aber dienstags und donnerstags trockne ich ab und am Wochenende wasche ich das Auto. Letztes Wochenende habe ich im Garten geholfen und staubgesaugt.
Ich bekomme 5 Pfund Taschengeld pro Woche und ich kaufe davon Zeitschriften und Süßigkeiten. Bei mir machen wir alle Hausarbeit! Meine Schwester kocht, mein Bruder geht einkaufen, meine Mutter bügelt und mein Vater wäscht die Wäsche.
Ich finde, 5 Pfund pro Woche Taschengeld ist nicht genug, weil ich meine eigene Kleidung kaufen muss. Aber meine Eltern sind arbeitslos. Schreib bald!
Dein(e)…

Effective revision or too much television?

Tante Inge's problem page

Tante Inge is a world expert on revision techniques for GCSE German. In this moving series of letters, published here for the first time, a young, frightened student seeks her advice on behalf of a 'friend' and finally gains a good grade in what was once her least favourite subject.

Dear Tante Inge,

I have a friend who is very worried about her German listening exam. She never understands a word her German teacher says and it's even worse when she listens to the cassette. What can she do to improve before the exam?

Concerned, Croydon.

Dear Tante Inge,

I told my friend what you said, and she says thanks very much, but she's no good at learning vocab. She looks at it very hard and it just won't go in. What should she do? Is there some magic way of getting it to stick?

Still Concerned, Croydon.

Dear Concerned,

How kind of you to take such an interest in your friend's progress! I am sure that you can help her if you give her the following advice. She does need to have a chat with her teacher about the problem, but there are things she can do to boost her confidence for the exam.

First of all, she should be spending five or ten minutes a day learning vocab. Little and often is the key to success! Secondly, she needs to listen to as much German as possible, so she should get hold of some German GCSE cassettes and listen to them over and over again until she understands most of what is being said.

Thirdly, when she's listening to her teacher, she should get into the habit of concentrating on the bits she does understand rather than the bits she doesn't recognise. Hope this does the trick!

Inge

Dear Still Concerned,

I wish I had friends like you! In answer to your question, yes there is a magic way of getting vocab to stick. In fact there are several ways. You have to make the words memorable, and to do that, you can, for example, draw little pictures to represent the meaning of the words. (Pictures are easier to remember than words.) Then you make a link in your mind between the picture and the word by looking at the picture and saying and/or writing the word over and over again.

Another useful tip would be for her to make connections in her mind with words she knows already in German or English. For example, she can remember **Hund** means *dog* because it looks like the English word *hound*.

The best advice of all is to get your friend to think of her own ways to learn vocab. Tell her to be as creative as possible, and she won't go far wrong.

Inge

Dear Tante Inge,

My friend just got full marks in a vocab test for the first time ever! I am really pleased for her. Not only that but she is feeling much more confident about understanding the teacher, and it's all thanks to you! I'm very grateful.

The only problem now is that she is very worried about the Speaking Test. She learns very hard for it and then her mind just goes blank. It's awful. I know you can help!

Hopeful, Croydon

Dear Tante Inge,

I PASSED!!

love, Ecstatic, Croydon xxx

Dear Hopeful,

I am delighted that your friend is so attentive to your advice, but why not suggest that she writes directly to me in future?

In the meantime you could tell her that preparing for the Speaking test means more than just learning very hard for it. If your friend is in the wrong state of mind at the time of the test, she may not do as well as she could.

The most important thing is that she learns how to relax. Ideally, she should have already perfected her technique several weeks before the test. Ask her to practise tensing and relaxing each muscle in her body until she can feel the tension draining away. Then she should create a mental image of a beautiful, peaceful place and imagine herself there. Any unwanted negative images can be mentally screwed into a ball and thrown away. As she explores her beautiful place, she should tell herself that she is feeling more and more relaxed. Try it yourself. It works.

There are, of course, other more traditional ways of relaxing. What's she into? Sport, singing, laughing – doing any of these things immediately before the test will give her a sense of well-being and, with any luck, a sense of proportion as well.

Inge

Ten fun ways to revise

- Practise your German on the good-looking Austrian student who's just moved in across the road.

- Intrigue the rest of your family by saying things in German that they don't understand.

- Challenge your mate to a vocab contest.

- Label everything in your bedroom in German.

- Talk to the dog in German. She won't criticise.

- Watch German films with your family. Tell them the subtitles are wrong.

- Go to a German-speaking country... and don't be shy.

- Organise a holiday in Cornwall – you'll meet lots of Germans.

- Put a new list of vocab on the inside of the loo door every week.

- Ask anyone who's going to Germany to get you some teenage magazines.

Index

Key: **00** = Memory Jogger

accidents   87, 88
activities
  everyday   **94**
  holiday   78–82
address   26
advertising   39
alphabet   19, **122**
animals   17, 22
appearance   16, 17, 21

bathroom   33, 34
bedroom   26
birthday   15, 16, 20, 21

café   71, 110
camping   83, 84
chemist   61, 62
cinema   36–38, 73, 74
clothes   18, 65, 66, **113**
colours   22, **106**
comparisons   20, 21, 62
complaints   70, 75–77
countries   79, **117**
coursework   12

dates   **101**
dictionaries   13, 128, 135
directions   59–61, **116**

exam grades   11–13
exam hints   13, 14, 146, 147

family   16, 20, **107**
food   33–35, 57–61, 71, **110**, **111**

going out/invitations   72–77

helping
  asking for   43, 44
  household tasks   29–31
hobbies   16
holidays   78–82, 90–92, **92**, **121**
home   26–28, **32**, **104**, **105**

illnesses   59–62, **114**, **115**
instructions   93
international world   **117**, **118**

languages   80, **118**
leisure activities   16–18, 43, 69, 70, **109**
letter writing   83
location   26

lost property   70

mealtimes   33–35, 43
modular course   12
music   35–37

nationalities   16, **116**, **117**
neighbourhood   62, 63
numbers   **102**

permission asking   68, 69
personality   16, 17, 20, 21
pets   17, 22
pocket money   29–31
postcards   90, 91
post office   63, 64

railway   89, **116**
reading   36–38
restaurant   75, 76
rooms   26–28
routine   41–43
rubrics   93

school   44–47, **119**, **120**
seasons   **101**
shopping
  clothes   64–66
  food   57–61
shops   60
spelling   19, 20
sport   69, 72, **109**
subjects   46, **119**
symbol techniques   18, 19
telephoning   53, 54
television   36–38
theft   70
tiers   11, 12
time
  frequency   30
  telling the   41–43, 100
town   62
transport   89
travel   42, **98**

visits   33–35

weather   84, 85, 92, **103**
word order   143, 144
work   49–53, 56, **97**
world environment   **96**

youth hostel   83, 84

BUZAN TRAINING COURSES

For further information on books, video and audio tapes, support materials and training courses, please send for our brochure.

Buzan Centres Ltd, 54 Parkstone Road, Poole, Dorset, BH15 2PX
Tel: 44 (0) 1202 674676, Fax: 44 (0) 1202 674776,
Email: Buzan_Centres_Ltd@compuserve.com